"The combination of theory, relevant personal reflection, and practical strategies make *The Neutrality Trap* a valuable resource for any practitioner serious about disrupting structural racism."

—**Cheryl L. Jamison,** J.D., Former Executive Director, Association for Conflict Resolution

"In *The Neutrality Trap*, Font-Guzmán and Mayer make the simple yet powerful point that neutrality–the North Star of dispute resolution processes–might serve more as an impediment than as an agent of social change. Having struck a heavy blow to the dispute resolution edifice, Font-Guzmán and Mayer help us rebuild it by guiding us on how to avoid the neutrality trap, engage in meaningful dialogue, and prepare to endure conflict. An important and timely contribution to the field."

—**Rafael Gely,** J.D., Ph.D., James E. Campbell Missouri Endowed Professor of Law, University of Missouri School of Law

"If you are a conflict resolution practitioner considering this book, you probably already know (or suspect) that insisting on neutrality in the face of systemic conflicts and prolonged injustices can do more harm than good. Bernie Mayer and Jackie Font-Guzmán move the conversation beyond a critique of neutrality. Drawing on their practical experiences, they offer an engaging, thought-provoking, and inspiring exploration of the ways we can use conflict resolution practices to engage enduring conflicts that require transformation rather than settlement."

—**Jayne Seminare** Docherty, Executive Director of the Center for Justice and Peacebuilding at EMU

"*The Neutrality Trap* brings clarity and hope to the dilemma so many of us mediators face these days: How to reconcile our commitment to peacemaking when our hearts are pulling us toward the social justice movements' cries for disruption. With wisdom and compassion Font-Guzmán and Mayer share their own experiences–professional and personal–to give us a framework for understanding today's polarization and a road map for moving forward. They model the honesty and vulnerability we all need to function in that intersection of conflict resolution and social justice reform."

—**Lucy Moore,** Author of *Common Ground on Hostile Turf*

"Read this book. It will take you into fertile, uncomfortable terrain as it dares to address the bitter divisions in America and beyond that, if unaddressed, will only fester and escalate. Dialogue is not enough. Mayer and Font-Guzmán take readers beyond easy prescriptions into difficult, necessary, and fruitful ways to engage and support structural social change. Read this book to change your mind. It can change your neighborhood. Read this book to change the world.

Though the field of conflict resolution has matured, practitioners have clung tenaciously to the cloak of neutrality, refusing to examine what it hides. Mayer and Font-Guzmán question who the cloak shelters in a world where systemic inequality is perpetuated too-often by conflict interventions. In a conversational narrative, the authors thoughtfully examine the vexing problems that the neutrality myth has obscured, challenging readers in nuanced ways. But they don't stop there. Nestled in a wide range of stories, they offer ways to advance fairness, equality, and justice. Their book is part challenge, part how-to-manual. It deserves to be widely read and applied with courage and heart."

—**Michelle LeBaron,** Professor and dispute resolution scholar | Peter A. Allard School of Law, The University of British Columbia

"Thank you for writing this. You've brought to light what is happening in the minds of social justice leaders and groups and have said it eloquently with much reflection. *The Neutrality Trap* makes me very hopeful for the future and I believe will encourage more people to step up and take an active role in the fight for systemic change."

—**Moya Mcalister,** Board Director of the Black Women of Forward Action (Windsor, ON)

"In *The Neutrality Trap*, Bernie Mayer and Jackie Font-Guzmán challenge conflict workers to rethink our role in dealing with the complex and oppressing social problems our society faces. The authors reflect on their previous work with remarkable frankness and humility, thereby helping the reader to see the problem with standing behind the comfortable shield of neutrality, and in so doing, failing to deal with unjust systems that create and perpetuate harm. They pick up this long-stalled topic and craft it into a call to reexamine how we see our role as conflict engagement practitioners and as citizens."

—**Susanne Terry,** Editor and contributor, *More Justice, More Peace: When Peacemakers are Advocates*

"Conflict specialists have long struggled with how to balance our role as dialogue facilitators with our commitment to expanding social justice. *The Neutrality Trap* explains how these two seemingly opposite roles can and must reinforce each other. The authors, Jackie Font-Guzmán and Bernie Mayer, describe their own journeys as intervenors and activists through truth-telling and fiercely honest self-examination. Social change is hard, and sometimes the hardest obstacles to overcome are hidden; this book challenges us to learn how to balance conflict and cooperation to overcome those obstacles in order to achieve real, sustainable social change."

—**Colin Rule,** CEO, Mediate.com and Arbitrate.com

THE
NEUTRALITY
TRAP

DISRUPTING AND CONNECTING
FOR SOCIAL CHANGE

BERNARD MAYER
JACQUELINE N. FONT-GUZMÁN

WILEY

Published by John Wiley & Sons, Inc., Hoboken, New Jersey.
Published simultaneously in Canada.

For general information on our other products and services or for technical support, please
contact our Customer Care Department within the United States at (800) 762-2974, outside the
United States at (317) 572-3993 or fax (317) 572-4002.

Wiley publishes in a variety of print and electronic formats and by print-on-demand. Some
material included with standard print versions of this book may not be included in e-books or
in print-on-demand. If this book refers to media such as a CD or DVD that is not included in
the version you purchased, you may download this material at http://booksupport.wiley.com. For
more information about Wiley products, visit www.wiley.com.

Library of Congress Cataloging-in-Publication Data available

ISBN 9781119793243 (Hardcover)
ISBN 9781119793274 (ePDF)
ISBN 9781119793410 (ePub)

Cover image: © Rawpixel/Getty Images
Author photos: Hope Moon and Howard Zehr
Cover design: Wiley

SKY10031939_121021

To the People of Puerto Rico—no matter where they are—whose fearless disruption of an oppressive colonial system and love for their nation keeps it alive;

and

to Daleep, born on November 6, 2021 and his parents, Sibyl and Jagjit. Daleep represents hope for the future and joy in the present.

contents

preface

"Raise your hand if you don't like Black people." The class laughed; the Black student targeted in this remark by one of her classmates was in shock—but not at a loss for words. When her teacher took her out of the room, asked her how she was doing and if she wanted to go home, she looked at her and called her out: "What are you going to do about the girl that made that remark in class? I am the only Black student in this class, she targeted me with that comment; what will you do about her? You've pulled me out of class like this problem was my fault. How does that look to the other students?" The teacher was planning to do nothing, it seems. The aggressor, a 9-year-old child (as was the target), was "just too young to be suspended, and probably did not understand the full meaning of what was being said." Nothing was said to the class, no discussion of why what happened was not okay, no effort to deal with the girl who made that remark.

Who was being protected? The aggressor? The other White students? The teacher? The school? The system? It's clear who was *not* being protected—a 9-year-old Black student who, along with so many others, experiences racism every day. This incident took place in Canada, but it could have happened anywhere. Racism is entrenched throughout our system, as is misogyny,

gender-based discrimination, xenophobia, and predatory capitalism. Our response as a society to these problems has by and large
been too little, too slow, and too performative. If we don't blame
the victims (which we often do), we focus on individual perpetrators, not on the systemic problems. We look for quick, facile solutions, a nice and neat end to the "conflict," so that we can move
on as quickly as possible.

Our Purpose

In this book, we look at what it takes for a system to change in
meaningful ways—what is required to dig deeply enough and
act decisively enough to make a genuine difference on the most
embedded, serious problems we face. We do so by looking at the
lessons we have learned at the intersection of our work as conflict interveners and social activists. In both roles, we have dealt
with intractable conflicts and systemic problems. In both, we have
worked at the intersection of individual actions, interpersonal
relationships, and enduring conflicts that have been with us for
years, even centuries. These problems will not simply disappear by
reaching an agreement or enacting a new policy. As important as
improved relationships, resolved conflicts, and good policies are,
they are not the same as changing systems embedded in values,
identity, power, and privilege.

We argue in this book that by promoting connections across
our differences, conflict intervention efforts can play an important role in social change. Approaches such as dialogue, facilitated
interactions, and restorative justice can be an integral part of struggles against oppression but only if they are in sync with concerted
efforts at system disruption. Dialogue for the sake of dialogue and
collaboration for the sake of collaboration, disconnected from a
commitment to social change, is likely to reinforce the *status
quo*. This is the *neutrality trap*. Unless our engagement efforts are
matched by an equally strong commitment to disrupting oppressive

systems, they will fail to make a profound contribution to social change. By trying to remain objective, neutral, impartial, and separate, conflict interveners and academics (along with many other professionals) reinforce system-maintaining norms, narratives, and practices that perpetuate a *status quo* that is calling out for change.

Disruption too is just part of the process of change. Effective social movements need to develop their capacity to participate in constructive engagement efforts as they continue to challenge the power structures that maintain systems of oppression. When and how to connect across our differences is an ongoing challenge because the energy and tactics necessary to disrupt systems can be at odds with the requirements for effective dialogue. How activists manage the tension between these two elements of the change process is a defining feature of how movements evolve and the success or failure of their efforts. Exploring how to navigate this practical challenge is a central theme of this book.

Another dynamic tension that social movements must be sensitive to is the difference between what we refer to as chaotic disruption and strategic disruption. *Chaotic disruption*—for example, when mass protests erupted after George Floyd's murder, the spontaneous demonstrations that led to the "Arab Spring," and the Stonewall riots in 1969—are essential to social change efforts because they mobilize support, attract a great deal of attention, and force reactions from those in power. But chaotic disruption is hard to sustain and difficult to keep clearly focused on the systemic nature of the problems they confront. *Strategic disruption*—for example, the ongoing actions of the civil rights, anti-nuclear, and environmental movements—keep the pressure on for systems change over time. They can go hand in hand with the building of sustainable organizational structures necessary for long-term efforts. But without the potential for chaotic disruption from time to time, their power is more easily circumscribed and even neutralized.

We explore these dynamics by looking at a wide range of both successful and faltering social change efforts, the analyses of activists and scholars, and our own experiences as conflict interveners and activists. We also discuss examples from the institutions and communities we belong to. Most of the stories we share are from public actions and interventions that we have been part of. Where we have discussed confidential matters, we have omitted or changed identifying information. We believe that these efforts, whether or not part of an organized movement, all have a role to play in promoting social change.

Our Perspectives

Of particular importance to us are the concepts and strategies that appear relevant to both the conflict engagement and the social change efforts we have been part of. We were determined not to fall into the neutrality trap. We believe that raising difficult issues and escalating conflict is necessary to understand our world and to bring about change. We do not hesitate to share our points of view, our values, and our commitments throughout this book. We think this increases the authenticity and value of what we have to say, but we also recognize that for some, this openness about our beliefs may call into question our credibility. We don't agree with that but appreciate that this will be easier to read for those already committed to anti-racist, anti-colonialist, pro-environment, and pro-egalitarian points of view. We hope others will find it stimulating and valuable as well.

Our thinking about these issues has developed over many years and is reflected in our previous writing. Bernie wrote *Beyond Neutrality* in 2004 to discuss the limits that conflict professionals place on their capacity to deal with the most important conflicts we face in our families, workplaces, communities, and society. These limits, he argued, stemmed from their focus on the role of the "neutral" and the goal of resolution. He expanded on this theme in *Staying with Conflict*, where he looked at the enduring nature of our most important conflicts, and in *The Conflict Paradox*. Bernie came to conflict work with a long background in the civil rights, anti-war, and environmental movements and as a labor union activist. His views have been informed by his background as a social worker, psychotherapist, and child of Holocaust survivors.

Jackie has long been concerned about racism, colonialism, and misogyny. In her book *Experiencing Puerto Rican Citizenship and Cultural Nationalism*, she discusses how Puerto Ricans experience and resist colonialism as they forge their national identity at the margin of the United States. Jackie has also written about how structures of oppression operate in the healthcare system and ways to create counter-narratives to transform (or dismantle) institutional and structural injustices. Jackie came to conflict work with a strong background as a healthcare administrator and a lawyer focusing on employment discrimination, civil rights, family law, and healthcare law. Her views have also been shaped by her experiences of being raised in Puerto Rico—a US colony—and countless conversations at the dinner table with her mother, who was a psychiatrist.

In all our work as professionals, trainers, teachers, and scholars, we have both been committed to being reflective practitioners. Our ideas are informed by our studies but are nurtured and tested in the cauldron of our practice experience, both as activists and interveners. This book is part of that conversation and will hopefully help others examine their own thinking, experiences, and practice in response.

Our Partnership

The two of us were colleagues for 15 years as faculty members of the Negotiation and Dispute Resolution Program at Creighton University (positions we have both now moved on from). At Creighton, we were allies in efforts to build an educational program that was attentive to long-term conflict engagement and system change and not just to transactional processes concerned with short-term solutions to enduring problems.

We decided to work as co-authors in the belief that a book of this nature requires a diversity of backgrounds. We also felt that our discussion had to continually return to questions of intersectionality, race, gender, and imperialism. Our partnership enabled us to do this by constantly holding ourselves and each other accountable for keeping our eyes on the major purpose and themes we had committed ourselves to.

Even though our partnership brings some diversity of ethnicity, age, gender, nationality, language of origin, professional training, and religious upbringing, for example, there are many elements of diversity we do not offer. We are both light-skinned, straight, cisgender, middle-aged or older, and from relatively privileged backgrounds (we explore this in Chapter 3). We recognize the limits of our perspective but its validity as well. We do not claim any special relevance because of our backgrounds, and, despite our best efforts, we know that we are likely to have exhibited our own implicit biases and limited understanding along the way. But we believe an awareness of that likelihood should not stop any of us from speaking our truths, sharing our insights, and telling our stories. If we were to allow this to restrain us from speaking in our authentic voices, we would be succumbing to the *neutrality trap* ourselves. We hope readers will be open to what we have to say and also keep in mind the limits of our perspectives.

How the Book Is Organized

We have organized this book into three broad sections:

- In Part I, "Engaging Conflict," we discuss the dynamic tension between engaging in conflict and disrupting systems (Chapter 1), what we mean by the neutrality trap and how to avoid it (Chapter 2), the critical role of race, gender, and intersectionality in social change (Chapter 3), and the potential and pitfalls of constructive engagement as an approach to social conflict (Chapter 4).

- In Part II, "Deepening Conflict," we look at the nature of long-term conflicts for which resolution is not a productive or reasonable goal (Chapter 5) and how to get beyond explanations of conflict and oppression focused on individual characteristics and behavior and delve more deeply into their systemic nature (Chapter 6).

- In Part III, "Strategic Disruption," we focus on the relationship between systemic and chaotic disruption and the role of nonviolent approaches to change (Chapter 7), and the role of alliances, teams, and leadership in social change (Chapter 8). We end with a forward look at disrupting and connecting for social change (Chapter 9).

We have used stories from long ago as well as recent examples, including events that took place while writing this book (e.g. the January 6, 2021, invasion of the US Capitol). We expect between today and its publication, new events will have occurred that will shed new light on our analysis and the stories we have shared. We want this book to be part of a dynamic, ongoing discussion and hope that we can all join in such a dialogue, one which we believe is critical to social change efforts.

—Bernie Mayer
Kingsville, Ontario

—Jackie N. Font-Guzmán
Harrisonburg, Virginia
October 30, 2021

part one

engaging conflict

chapter one

engaging and disrupting for social change

"Freedom is not a state; it is an act. It is not some enchanted garden perched high on a distant plateau where we can finally sit down and rest. Freedom is the continuous action we all must take, and each generation must do its part to create an even more fair, more just society."

—John Lewis, *Across That Bridge: A Vision for Change and the Future of America*

At a time when our country and our world seem constantly on the precipice of chaos and disaster, we can easily lose faith that the future has anything to offer other than more and worse of the same. Fires rage, hurricanes destroy, pandemics kill, and we seem incapable of doing anything about them. Our political systems seem much better at redistributing wealth upward, maintaining the power of elites, and suppressing dissent than confronting our most serious challenges. Democracy seems in retreat and authoritarianism on the rise across the globe.

But pessimism itself contributes to our political paralysis, and we must never forget that systems do change, people's lives improve,

3

and oppressive governments fall. We are on a long and winding road that takes us to some very surprising, sometimes wonderful, but also frightening places.

Sometimes change is painfully slow, and sometimes advances are undone. Then, suddenly, amazing and important moral progress occurs. What were once unusual and unpopular attitudes about same-sex marriage, gender fluidity, and sexuality rapidly become far more widely accepted. A totalitarian system that has held millions of people under its thumb suddenly disintegrates. While racism continues to affect every corner of our societies, racist ideology is broadly rejected by growing numbers of people.

But none of these changes occur magically or without significant pain, and all are vulnerable to the immense capacity of systems of power and privilege to defend themselves and claw back progress toward fundamental change. For broadly based and deeply rooted progressive change to occur and for power structures that maintain an oppressive social order to be upended, those systems must be *disrupted—something must occur that forces them to change how they operate.* The disruption may be unplanned and external (e.g. climate or demographic changes) or intentional and directed (e.g. social movements or political campaigns). The seeds of change are embedded in all organic systems, and that includes oppressive systems that seek to maintain a destructive status quo. How they change, however, is not only not foreordained but largely unpredictable. Yet change will happen, and we will necessarily be part of it.

Strategic Disruption

No matter how dramatic the impetus from external sources, intentional efforts at disruption through popular movements and political activism are essential to forcing change and guiding how it occurs. Without intentionality and a conscious change strategy, our capacity to foster system reconstruction (and, in some cases, system destruction) is limited and haphazard. Each of us has a role to play in this, and we each have a unique set of capacities that we can bring to this process. In order to do so, we have to recognize this potential individually and collectively and find the moral courage to pursue it.

One place to start is by recognizing how often, despite our best intentions, especially when we occupy positions of privilege, we are part of the problem. Much of what we do, including much of the good work we undertake, contributes to the maintenance of systems that we want to change. This is inevitable because we are part of these systems. Our natural desire to believe that we are good people doing good things can lead us to downplay our role in maintaining the structures of oppression and hierarchy.

This paradox—that the good work we do often reinforces destructive systems—can be found in what conflict interveners do to guide disputes toward resolution, but the same is true for all "service professions," including medicine, counseling, law, human services, and education.

For example:

- When we participate in collaborative efforts to deal with organizational conflict, we may be enabling the continuance of an exploitative hierarchy.

- When we foster dialogue between community members and police officers to try to improve relationships and communication, we may be reinforcing a public safety model that emphasizes law enforcement over community development and mental health.

- When we convene conversations among different ethnic groups to try to resolve tensions that have led to violent interchanges, we may undercut a growing movement to promote the rights of a historically exploited group.

None of these efforts are necessarily misguided or inappropriate. As we seek to change systems, we also have to support people as they navigate these systems. But undertaking them without considering the impact our well-intentioned and even necessary actions may play in the larger pattern of dominance, oppression, or hierarchy is problematic and sometimes dangerous. One of the most important challenges we face in promoting social change is how to develop strategies for increasing constructive dialogue among groups in conflict while also raising the level of that conflict in an effective and durable way.

Disrupting and Engaging

Many of us who have worked in the conflict field (e.g. as facilitators, mediators, peace builders, and trainers) also have backgrounds as social activists where raising the prominence of public conflict is central to the mission of promoting justice. Working to help people resolve their differences has often seemed like a logical and constructive next step. But what seemed like a natural progression has often meant losing the clarity of purpose that the previous focus on social change had provided. While the conflict intervention field has at times helped consolidate changes that social movements have generated, it has also sometimes undercut the energy necessary to build movements by focusing prematurely on dialogue, de-escalation, and resolution.

The two of us have spent a significant part of our professional lives working to understand what drives conflict; the relationship between communication, emotion, power, culture, and structure; and the processes that can be used to support people in working through their conflicts in a constructive way. We have guided public dialogues, high-stakes negotiations, and intense interpersonal interactions in organizations, communities, and families. Much of our work has involved trying to identify how people can resolve differences, arrive at solutions to seemingly intractable problems, and lower the level of tension and hostility in volatile situations. But in doing so we have also had to support people in raising difficult issues, accepting that some elements of their most important conflicts are not amenable to tangible short-term solutions, and learning to mobilize and use their power effectively.

We have experienced some astonishingly and unexpected transformative moments in our work with others, but we know that profound change does not come easily, predictably, or by the mechanistic application of some formula for human interaction. We believe that just as the lessons we have learned as advocates for social change have informed our work as conflict interveners, our work on conflict sheds light on the struggle for social justice. What those lessons are and how they can be applied to the volatile world we inhabit is the focus of this book.

Three of the most important lessons we have learned are the vital role of conflict in breaking cycles of oppression, the importance of taking a strategic approach to long-term conflict, and the danger that neutrality poses as a central guiding principle for the role that conflict interveners play in the change process. These lessons are relevant not only to conflict specialists but to all those working for social change.

Constructive Conflict

Conflict intervention practitioners frequently assert that conflict itself is not the problem, but how we handle it often is. Labor and management struggle over competing interests, environmentalists and fossil fuel producers look at the world through different lenses, and divorcing parents often have different visions and values about rearing children. The challenge we all face, therefore, is not so much how to resolve these differences but how to find a constructive way to deal with them over time.

What conflict interveners have usually meant by handling conflict constructively, however, has been about bringing these differences to rapid and peaceful resolution, tamping down the level of emotionality and particularly anger, "separating the people from the problem," and minimizing the disruptive effects of conflict on people, communities, and institutions. This vision of what makes conflict constructive negates the true importance of creative and constructive conflict in our world.

So what makes conflict truly constructive?

Constructive conflict moves us forward in creating the world we want to be part of, one that reflects our most important values and desires, promotes the systems that will contribute to the changes we seek, and disrupts those that interfere with these. Constructive conflict is also carried on in accordance with our values about human and group interaction and with the fundamental goals we are pursuing.

There are two important caveats here, however. One is that what is constructive is contextual to the person and situation. The other is that no action is pure. The line between constructive conflict and pointless destruction is often a fine one. When does angry, militant, and effective mass action turn into looting, arson, and violence against individuals?

The initial reaction to the George Floyd murder was justified, necessary, chaotic, and sometimes destructive of the very communities who have been historically victimized by the White racist system that the protests were directed against. This is not unusual. It is what happened after Rodney King was beaten, Dr. King was assassinated, and during some of the most important labor actions in American history (e.g. the Pullman and Homestead Strikes). Accepting that such violence may be an inevitable and sometimes energizing aspect of social change efforts may force many of us to deal with an uncomfortable level of cognitive dissonance, but working for social change requires that we do so. Of course, the violence associated with progressive social movements, although generally small in scale and destruction, is frequently exaggerated and seized upon to discredit these movements in their entirety. This was the response of many supporters of Donald Trump who tried to minimize the destruction and danger posed by the invasion of the US Capitol on January 6, 2021, by equating it with the minor acts of violence that occurred during some Black Lives Matter protests.

The challenge in developing a truly constructive approach to conflict, which of necessity is disruptive, is to move through periods of chaotic disruption to build a multi-pronged, sustainable, strategic, nonviolent approach to disrupting oppressive systems.

Nonviolence and Disruption

As may be obvious, nonviolence is one key to sustainable approaches to systems disruption. Nonviolence as both a philosophy and a strategy has been at the heart of many of the most important and successful social movements in recent history. The anti-nuclear, civil rights, women's, gay rights, and environmental movements have largely adhered to a commitment to nonviolence. This has been essential to sustaining them and to harnessing the moral power that has been vital to their success.

But we should remember that the power of nonviolence lies not only in its moral consistency and vision but in what lurks behind it. The alternative to taking seriously the grievances expressed by nonviolent protestors is often chaotic and destructive violence. This was true of the movement against British Colonialism led by Mohandas Gandhi, the struggle to end apartheid in South Africa, and the US civil rights movement. We should also remember that in a White supremacist system, people of color are held to a very different standard about violence than White people.

At the opening of the Livonia Trial in 1964, Nelson Mandela discussed why after years of a disciplined commitment to nonviolence, he chose to participate in acts of sabotage against the apartheid regime of South Africa:

> "All lawful modes of expressing opposition to this principle had been closed by legislation, and we were placed in a position in which we had either to accept a permanent state of inferiority, or to defy the Government. We chose to defy the Government. We first broke the law in a way which avoided any recourse to violence; when this form was legislated against, and when the Government resorted to a show of force to crush opposition to its policies, only then did we decide to answer violence with violence."
>
> (Mandela, Statement at the opening of his trial on charges of sabotage, Supreme Court of South Africa, 1964)

Mandela never disavowed this decision, albeit one he was very loath to make. Whether this was the wisest or most effective approach remains an interesting question. The group that engaged in sabotage (Umkhonto—an offshoot of the ANC) was quickly broken up, and these actions led to the long imprisonment of Mandela and his associates. Directly, it did little to disrupt the apartheid system. But 27 years later, Mandela emerged from imprisonment as a widely respected leader who was able to negotiate an end to apartheid and take the critical initial steps to building a new society. His power was in part derived from the widespread recognition that he was perhaps the only one with the credibility to enter into an agreement that would not be immediately rejected or provoke mass outbreaks of violence.

Recognizing that the power of nonviolence lies to some extent in the alternative it provides to a more violent confrontation does not mean that proponents of nonviolence are hypocritical. Effective movements for social change, as noted above, are not pristine or rigidly consistent.

Resolution, Engagement, and Disruption

Social movements inevitably face difficult strategic decisions about how to interface with the people they are hoping to influence and the systems that they want to change. Activists must choose whether to focus on disrupting systems, engaging with those whose beliefs and behaviors they oppose, or looking for potential areas of agreements that may be steps, even small ones, on the road to change. Whatever the immediate focus, over time all three approaches—disruption, engagement, and resolution—are necessary elements to the change process. An element of each is almost always present no matter what fundamental strategy a movement or group has adopted.

As conflict interveners, we often think about resolution as the be-all and end-all goal and consider constructive engagement as a positive step along the road to resolution. We tend to view disruption as a problem to overcome through engagement and resolution. However, in the search for social change we may have it backward. Resolution efforts are often most important as steps along a path that leads to system disruption. The civil rights movement, for example, was built on incremental changes, such as the integration of lunch counters and bus systems, but each of these contributed to the development of a network of diverse relationships that facilitated the expansion of the effort to change more fundamental elements in the system such as the distribution of political power. Resolution of deeply rooted conflicts will not occur without disruption.

Genuine engagement most often builds on a foundation of disruption and at the same time requires an openness to identifying areas of agreement. On the other hand, for disruption to be effective it must also open the door to engagement and resolution. Even if the goal of disruption is to dismantle a system, such as colonialism, engagement is essential. Effective movements respect the interdependence as well as the tension between these three strategic goals.

Mohandas Gandhi and the Salt March

Mohandas Gandhi was a master of disruption. One of the most important events in the struggle for Indian independence from the British Empire was the Salt March of 1930 (History.com Editors 2020). The Salt March was undertaken to protest the repressive and racist policy restricting who could manufacture or collect salt, but it was also an all-encompassing protest against colonialism. Thousands of Indians joined with Gandhi on a 240-mile march to the Arabian Sea where in defiance of the law they collected salt from tidal deposits. Gandhi was one of over 60,000 people who were arrested. This action exposed the viciousness and racism of British imperialism and led to widespread condemnation. Disruption occurred.

But what happened after Gandhi was released from prison about 7 months later (in January 1931)? Gandhi met with Lord Irwin, the Viceroy of India, and agreed to call off his nonviolent campaign in exchange for being provided an "equal" negotiating role at a conference on the future of India to be held in London later that year. The conference did not produce any significant agreements, but it established Gandhi and more importantly the movement that he led as an inescapable force that could not be ignored. More disruption followed (civil disobedience, repeated arrests, hunger strikes, mass demonstrations). More engagement and negotiations occurred as well. India achieved independence in 1947, but the struggle against the continued effects of colonialism, the caste system, and racism continue.

Disrupting Systems of Oppression

Challenging systems that perpetuate oppression can be overwhelming, especially for those who bear the brunt of the oppression and may feel simultaneously responsible for advancing change and disempowered—a dilemma that Emily Martin (1994, 122) has called "empowered powerlessness." Where to even begin? And once we disrupt the system, what is next? How do we move from awareness to disruption and then to change?

Recognizing the importance of disruption is an important first step in refocusing from system maintenance to social change. Disruptions can be overt and group based, such as organizing social movements, unionizing, or taking to the streets to demand change. Other approaches are more individual, such as calling in someone when they engage in a microaggression (an exchange that denigrates and insults a specific person or group (Sue 2010, 5)), kneeling for a national anthem, writing an op-ed, or raising concerns about implicit bias with colleagues or managers.

Disruption is successful when it calls attention to routinized acts of violence and oppression and causes systems to reorganize in a way that limits or eliminates these acts. Sometimes when we challenge everyday microaggressions, we interrupt the normalization of the assumptions, prejudices, and injustices that enable such aggressions and, in doing so, we may create openings for dialogue where we thought none were possible (Cohen and Strand 2021).

During the summer of 2019, I (Jackie) joined Puerto Ricans who, for 14 days, took to the streets with a self-organized movement that ousted Ricardo (Ricky) Rosselló, the governor of Puerto Rico. Rosselló announced his resignation on July 24, 2019, one day after close to a million people (a third of Puerto Rico's population) shut down the island by occupying the main expressway in San Juan and demanded his resignation.

The tipping point for this insurrection was the publication of 889 pages of texts from a messaging app administered

(Continued)

(*Continued*)

by Rosselló. The chat included his closest advisers, a lobbyist, and cabinet members—all 12 of whom were men. The chat contained expletive-laced attacks on the LGBTQIA+ community, women, obese individuals, the 4,645 people who died during Hurricane María, political opponents, members of the governor's own political party, journalists, and the poor. Rosselló became a symbol of the corruption, inequity, and colonial oppression that has plagued Puerto Rico for centuries. This protest was a manifestation of a conflict rooted in over 500 years of colonization, embedded in Puerto Rico's complex interactions with the United States, and wrapped in the island's national identity and cultural values.

Puerto Ricans' expression of their culture gave life, power, and unity to the movement. Puerto Ricans ousted the governor through dancing, painting, poetry, acrobatics, kayaking, scuba diving, skydiving, singing, motorcycling, horseback riding, biking, pot banging, kite flying, improvisational comedy—and more. The arts and humanities took over the land, water, air, and space in Puerto Rico.

We have seen similar efforts to confront oppression and authoritarianism in Hong Kong, Myanmar, Chile, Russia, and elsewhere. In each case, the pushback was significant and has led to violence, mass arrests, and an increase in the repressive nature of the regime.

In the face of such ferocious resistance, it is easy to become disillusioned about the possibility of progress against oppression. These upheavals are manifestations of how in the face of enduring conflicts creative approaches to conflict escalation can move systems toward democracy and inclusion. But progress does not occur in a neat, linear, unidirectional way, and we can hold no certainty about end results or unintended consequences.

Of course, not all social movements are aimed at confronting oppression or injustice. Some movements (e.g. the Tea Party or the Proud Boys) are intended to maintain privilege and dominance. The efforts to subvert the outcome of the 2020 presidential election in the United States were the expression of resistance to the empowerment of women and minorities. The struggles between progressive and regressive forces are ancient and enduring, and the struggle for justice is powerful but not straightforward.

Acting Small, Dreaming Big

Beverly Daniel Tatum (2017, 340–341) argues that the antidote for feeling despair when confronting injustice is to focus our energy on our "sphere of influence." What and whom can we influence? What are small actions under our control that can lead to fulfilling a dream of a beloved community? How can we expand and strengthen our network? How can we build community? How can we best use our talents? Acting small means using our agency, as limited as it may be at times, to its strategic maximum while keeping our focus on the dream that motivated us in the first place. If we are part of the system, then we can change the system by changing how we behave within the system.

A popular environmental slogan (still seen on many bumper stickers) from about 30 years ago—Think Globally, Act Locally—conveys both a vision and strategy. To understand the scale of the challenge posed by global warming, species extinction, extreme weather, and other environmental disasters, we have to take a global perspective. But how do we promote an effective approach to these challenges? We need a movement with a global vision and a local presence.

For example, how do we combat an economic system that has led to increasing economic inequality? How do we contend with the rise of authoritarian populism? What about nativism, racism, misogyny, imperialism? All of these are global phenomena.

The rise of Donald Trump is not disconnected from that of Victor Orban in Hungary, Rodrigo Duterte in the Philippines, or Jair Bolsonaro in Brazil. The global dimensions of these challenges must be understood if movements for change are to flourish. But building effective movements for change requires local action, local leaders, and a focus on local manifestations of global problems. Global networks are important, as are global spokespersons, but the real work takes place in our local communities and organizations where the focus may be affordable housing, police-community relationships, or sexual misconduct at a local high school.

This is related to a central challenge that mediators are very familiar with: How do you connect the underlying concerns or issues that people are trying to come to grips with in conflict, to the tangible manifestations of them that tend to be foremost in their thoughts and emotions?

Divorced parents may be in conflict over how to share time with their children over Christmas or which school they should attend or where they should spend every other Wednesday night, but these details almost always represent more basic concerns about parenting, decision making, boundaries, and communication.

A neighborhood that is up in arms about plans to locate a homeless shelter nearby may be worried about safety and property values, and there are likely racial biases at work as well. But the focus of discussion instead is usually on parking, traffic, lighting, and design. Almost always, the most strenuous arguments start out about the specifics, but the real problem lies at a deeper or more systemic level. Pretending it is just about traffic and safety can enable racist policies, but ignoring those concerns can prevent genuine engagement from occurring. This challenge is not just about the geographical reach or expression of a conflict. It also involves the systemic versus behavioral view, the immediate concerns versus the long-term challenge, individual action versus communal responsibility, and the action of groups versus that of leaders. Social movements must find a way to attend to the immediate and local while maintaining a long-term and far-reaching focus.

Disrupting for What: A Guiding Vision

> Dr. King's Beloved Community is a global vision in which all people can share in the wealth of the earth. In the Beloved Community, poverty, hunger, and homelessness will not be tolerated because international standards of human decency will not allow it. Racism and all forms of discrimination, bigotry, and prejudice will be replaced by an all-inclusive spirit of sisterhood and brotherhood. In the Beloved Community, international disputes will be resolved by peaceful conflict-resolution and recon- ciliation of adversaries, instead of military power. Love and trust will triumph over fear and hatred. Peace with justice will prevail over war and military conflict.
>
> —The King Center, n.d.

> Democratic socialists believe that both the economy and society should be run democratically—to meet public needs, not to make profits for a few. To achieve a more just society, many structures of our government and economy must be radically transformed through greater economic and social democracy so that ordi- nary Americans can participate in the many decisions that affect our lives . . .
>
> Democratic socialists do not want to create an all- powerful government bureaucracy. But we do not want big corporate bureaucracies to control our society either. Rather, we believe that social and economic decisions should be made by those whom they most affect.
>
> —Democratic Socialists of America, 2020

Social movements are often accused of being clearer about what is wrong and must change than about their vision for the future. This is mostly an undeserved criticism because it's impossible to know precisely how large-scale systems will reorganize or to predict the future. We have to start with an understanding of what is not working now. Nonetheless, the development of a sense of what kind of society or world we want is essential to powerful change efforts, as is a roadmap for how to get there.

During the first half of the 20th century (and earlier), progressive movements were often motivated by a vision of society founded in socialist ideology. But, particularly in the United States, socialism (mostly unfairly) became associated with support for authoritarian regimes and with intrusive governmental bureaucracies. For much of the last 50 years, socialist ideology has not provided the motivating vision it once did. However, more recently, especially with the presidential campaigns of Bernie Sanders, the ideology of Democratic Socialism has seen a revival. Nonetheless as seen in the last US election, associating a cause (universal healthcare or the Green New Deal, for example) or a politician with socialism continues to be an effective tactic for those seeking to resist change.

Martin Luther King's vision of a Beloved Community has been an important source of strength for the civil rights and Black Lives Matter movements. The Beloved Community provides a picture of a non-exploitative, nonviolent society, but it says little about the social, political, and economic arrangements that would actualize and sustain this vision. Dr. King believed that a radical commitment to nonviolence and social justice was the path to putting this vision into practice.

There has been no shortage of other contending visions and ideologies: anarchism, liberation theology, radical feminism, and communitarianism, to name a few. It's not our purpose to suggest what vision should or will take hold. Our sense is that ultimately some of the values and ideas of many of these ideologies will have to be part of the long-term vision of progressive movements if they are to address the challenges we face at their most fundamental level.

What seems clear is that having a hopeful but realistic vision of the world we are striving for, a vision that takes us beyond our immediate struggles or particular focus, is part of what makes fundamental change possible. Such a vision is more likely if we can point to societies that have had at least some success in walking down this road. We can look to social democratic systems (e.g. Sweden or Finland) or countries that have achieved some success in pursuing multiculturalism (e.g. New Zealand or Canada) as partial examples. But these are not perfect examples because they are culturally specific models that will not necessarily work in other contexts, are themselves flawed, and were not designed to deal with problems that are truly global in scale.

This lack of a clear and comprehensive vision for social movements is also in some respects a good thing. Rigid ideologies or movements that have attached themselves to the example of a particular society (China, Cuba, or the Soviet Union, for example) have failed to provide an effective vision, have been political failures, and most importantly have ended up being morally compromised.

Instead, we need to think of a long-term vision as a process rather than an outcome. The search for a comprehensive vision that is consistent with our values, connected to our actions, and hopeful but also realistic is an essential part of effective social movements. Such a search must be iterative, informed by experience and values, based on a continuous effort to understand our social, political, and economic systems, and inclusive of diverse people and communities.

The following chapters look at both the obstacles we face and strategies we can employ to promote social change. The book focuses on three essential challenges, which together form the steppingstones for system change: productive approaches to conflict engagement, deepening conflict, and system disruption. We start by considering a significant ideological cultural obstacle posed by the intellectual foundation that informs the work of many professions and institutions, including that of conflict interveners and the justice system—the ideology of neutrality.

Reflective Dialogue: What Keeps Us Going

Writing a book of this nature requires an ongoing reflective process. Both of us have carried this on individually but also together as we have sought to consolidate our thinking about how social conflict can unfold in a powerful and meaningful way. We have drawn on all that we have learned from our own practice as students and practitioners of conflict engagement and from our history as activists. We will end some chapters with a brief dialogue between us about how our thinking has evolved and what this has meant for our work on conflict and social change.

Bernie: Jackie, as we prepared different drafts of this chapter, each of us discussed the tension between being realistic about the difficulty of achieving profound social change while remaining optimistic about the profound power of collective action to change society. I have often said that optimism is a moral obligation, but optimism that is not grounded in a realistic view of the challenges we face is neither authentic nor useful. Integrating optimism and realism is an ongoing personal and professional challenge. What I find helps, in fact is required, is to embrace uncertainty. We don't know for sure what the future holds; we know we face real challenges, and to be convinced all will be well makes no sense—but neither does being sure that all is lost and we are doomed. I hold onto both uncertainty and a lifetime of experience in seeing people, groups, and societies change in response to social action. What is your take on the potential to disrupt, dismantle, rebuild, and sustain healthier and more just social structures?

Jackie: Bernie, I have never given up hope that we can create systems and institutional structures in which we can share and celebrate our common humanity. When I look back at what moves me and sustains my hope, it always comes down to love—the love that allows me to be present for others, see the unseen, and disrupt spaces in which injustice has been normalized. During my litigation years in Puerto Rico, a significant part of my practice was representing (in non-criminal cases) clients who were involuntarily or voluntarily confined in custodial, correctional, healthcare, or penal institutions. I made many visits to these institutions to meet with my clients. I never imagined I could see and experience so much love in a system that was ingrained with so much violence and abuse.

One rainy morning, as I was driving to the parking area of a penal institution, I saw a woman trudging up the hill clutching a stuffed paper bag. (Lawyers could drive up the hill, other visitors had to walk about a quarter of a mile.) She was probably in her late 50s, had no umbrella, and was wearing a worn-out dress. It looked like the real weight she was carrying was the one on her shoulders. I remember feeling sadness and indignation while thinking—she is most likely someone's mother or grandmother. Her exhaustion and pain were evident, but so was her love. She, unknowingly, made me see the injustice of institutional procedures that hindered the ability of prisoners to be visited by their loved ones. It was also a reminder of our interconnectedness; no matter how much unjust structures try to "place people out of sight," we are all still connected. Seeing with love is what allows me

(Continued)

(*Continued*)

to feel the indignation that moves me toward confronting unjust systems and building more just social structures.

Bernie, doing this work is difficult, emotionally draining, and many times is unappreciated. What moves you to persevere?

Bernie: For me too, the love, caring, and connectedness that are at the heart of social movements are important sources of hope and energy. But I also feel that sometimes anger at what I see happening is an important motivator as well. We are told in so many ways that profound change is hopeless—that racism has always been with us and always will be, that inequality is inevitable, that climate change can't be avoided so we should just adapt (or deny), and that our actions of resistance are only going to be met by powerful pushback. It sometimes seems safer to be pessimistic and cynical than hopeful. That really makes me angry. I refuse to give in to hopelessness. But this is not just an emotional reaction. I really do believe that progress will be made.

We are in the midst of the COVID-19 pandemic that has brought a sense of gloom and pessimism to all of us. The election that we have just been through, the concerted and frightening efforts that have been taken to call into question the results that ousted a would-be dictator, and the incredible numbers of voters who supported him despite his overt racism, authoritarianism, misogyny, and incompetence are all reasons to have doubts about our future.

But many more people rejected than supported Trump. We voted him out. Democracy somehow survived. We are going to find our way through COVID-19, although not without having paid an awful price, and the responses to voter suppression, to the killing of people of color, and to the threats to our climate have laid the ground for what I hope will be a sustained movement for change.

I love your story about the woman who had to trudge up the hill. It feels like a metaphor for our time. We all are trudging, some with more privilege and power than others. Our obligation is to come together to help everyone get up that hill.

How has COVID-19, the election, and its aftermath affected you?

Jackie: I like that you raise anger as a catalyst for change and a motivator to organize. Many times, anger is a path to restoring social justice. I am always disappointed (and angered) when people do not get angry or are indifferent when confronted with injustices. My grandmother used to say that when you lose your capacity to become indignant, you might as well be dead. I believe anger is one of those emotions that we shut down too quickly. As conflict practitioners and activists, an effective way to escalate conflict is by channeling anger toward indignation, a truly powerful emotion.

The elections and COVID-19 have taken me to places of fear, anxiety, anger, rage, frustration, solidarity, hope, joy, compassion, and reflection. At the intersection of COVID-19 and the US election we have witnessed how deeply racism, both individual and systemic, is embedded in our society. Hispanics, people of color, and Indigenous populations are dying at a higher rate than other groups. COVID-19 has debunked the myth that the United States has the best healthcare in the world by evidencing how fragile our health system is. It is distressing that I live in a wealthy nation where people have to set up GoFundMe accounts to raise money to cover their

(*Continued*)

(Continued)

healthcare costs. It has been tragic to see the politicization of sound public health guidelines such as wearing masks or getting vaccinated.

The historical period in which we live has shown the fragility and, at times, hollowness of the US democracy. Can we say we live in a democracy when so many people are excluded from participating in the decision-making process of policies that directly affect them? Can we say that the United States is a democracy when it does not advance political self-determination processes in all the colonies it possesses? It feels like the empire is crumbling and we are adrift in the turbulence that its dissolution is creating. Many of these systems cannot be fixed because they are not broken. They are working as they were intended to operate by privileging certain groups at the expense of others. And this is where my emotions shift toward hope and reflecting on how much work we need to do, together, if we want to advance democracy and disrupt oppressive systems.

How has it been for you to witness the amplification of polarization in the US elections as a dual US and Canadian citizen, residing in Canada?

Bernie: This period has definitely tested my sense of who I am. My Canadian self is very happy to be spending this time isolating in Canada and feeling insulated not only from the COVID-19 chaos in the United States (we have our struggles with it here too) but also from the polarization and seeming hopelessness of rallying the US people to face our most pressing problems. But my US self cares deeply about what is happening across the border. I believe it is not really polarization that is our most daunting political problem but the lack of a unifying vision about how we can deal with our seemingly insurmountable challenges. This requires building an effective movement for change with a clear vision for the future. I think such a movement will do more to create constructive conversations and break through polarization than anything else we can do.

What about you? How does your Puerto Rican self make sense of what is happening in the United States?

Jackie: One of the sad advantages of being from a colony is that we have seen and experienced firsthand the many ways that oppression manifests itself. Therefore, my Puerto Rican self is not surprised by what is happening in the United States. However it does give me hope that more and more people in the United States may be willing to start engaging in conversations that they would not have imagined having five years ago. In my opinion, racism is not the root cause of what is currently happening in the United States; rather it is the US imperialist mindset that has fueled racism and White supremacy. As a Puerto Rican, I am hopeful that as conversations about dismantling racism continue to take place, more people in the United States will start grappling with the harsh reality that they are an empire and as such, they continue to own colonies and deprive people of democracy. Maybe the conversations in the United States can advance a self-determination process for Puerto Rico, all the other US colonies, and for Indigenous nations.

chapter two

the neutrality trap

"If you are neutral in situations of injustice, you have chosen the side of the oppressor. If an elephant has its foot on the tail of a mouse and you say that you are neutral, the mouse will not appreciate your neutrality."

—Desmond Tutu

We began drafting this chapter during the first week of 2021. Then the invasion of the US Capitol happened. The biggest threat to American democratic institutions in our lifetime, it grew out of a racist and nativist streak that is foundational to US culture. It also grew out of a strain of that culture that asserts that only White Christian fundamentalists really count and that those who did not vote for Trump, especially people of color, are not real Americans. Those who enabled Trump's actions bought into his false and dangerous narratives about the validity of the election and refused to take any responsibility for the violence, destruction, and attack on democracy that occurred. They have since urged that we "move on" and argued that our focus should now be on unity and reconciliation (c.f. Wang 2021). But reconciliation without responsibility taking or accountability is no reconciliation at all.

Not surprisingly, the response of many in the conflict field to the attack was to call for more dialogue, preferably overseen by trained third-party mediators, to heal our wounds (see Kenneth Cloke FB post of Jan. 9, 2021). But dialogue is not just an academic exchange of views. It requires a serious effort to achieve a deeper understanding in service of moving toward a better future. Healing requires acceptance that harm has been done, reparations may be needed, and change is necessary. Dialogue in the absence of such a commitment reinforces the status quo.

In a very emotional and moving discussion of her experience during the invasion of the Capitol, Congresswoman Alexandria Ocasio-Cortez revealed that she is a survivor of sexual assault. She explained what she felt it takes to move on:

> "So many of the people who helped perpetrate . . . what happened in the Capitol are trying to tell us all to move on . . . to forget about what happened . . . [and] that it wasn't a big deal . . . without any accountability, without any truth-telling, or without actually confronting the extreme damage, physical harm, loss of life, and trauma that was inflicted on not just me as a person, not just other people as individuals, but on all of us as a collective, and on many other people. We cannot move on without accountability. We cannot heal without accountability. And so all of these people who want to tell us to move on are doing so at their own convenience . . . . These are the tactics that abusers use . . . . What they're asking for when they say, 'Can we just move on?' is . . . 'Can we just forget this happened so that I can do it again, without recourse?'"
>
> (Alexandria Ocasio-Cortez, Instagram Live video, 2021)

The Limits of Dialogue

After the shock of the election of Donald Trump in 2016, many progressives, especially many conflict practitioners, argued that Trump supporters had to be heard, their concerns needed to be taken seriously, and earnest efforts at dialogue between those who supported him and those who opposed his election were essential.

A variety of efforts were made to organize listening sessions and interchanges. Some of these were productive. Efforts to understand the lives, thinking, and genuine concerns of Trump's supporters have occasionally been worthwhile (see, for example, *The Forgotten* by Ben Bradlee Jr., 2018, and also see Chapter 6 for further discussion) and their legitimate concerns should be taken seriously. But there is something about these efforts that misses an important point and feels patronizing. As important as it is to listen, listening alone can be counterproductive without the inclusion of the voice of the oppressed and others who disagree with Trump's policies.

Often, listening is the easy and safe part of communicating across divides. The more difficult part is to speak our hard but essential truths, truths that we know may escalate conflict, and doing so in a way that encourages others to try to understand us. The first step to ensuring meaningful dialogue is finding our voice and developing the power that allows us to speak with confidence that we will not just be dismissed and to support others to do the same. Speaking with power and listening with curiosity and openness are twin sides of meaningful dialogue.

When there is a significant difference in power, as between police and an African American community, even well-intended dialogue can easily reinforce the inequality that exists. The process itself tends to have both implicit and explicit rules of engagement that favor the most powerful. For example, the expectations that only one person speak at a time, that the focus be on the future, not the past, and that emotions, particularly anger, be toned down are most congruent with the norms of those in power. As a result, everyone may listen to each other but then return to their relative positions of power and powerlessness, and little will change.

Those of us who organize and conduct these events can easily think that something important has happened, abetted by our commitment to hearing everybody in an open-minded way. But what won't have happened is an effort to genuinely challenge power differentials and the systems that reinforce these. Instead, we may well have misdirected the energies of the disempowered from organizing for change to understanding the privileged—something they are likely to have had considerable experience in doing. We have fallen into the neutrality trap.

There are professional and personal dimensions to this. Neutrality, impartiality, objectivity, and independence are values that many of us proclaim as a sign of our professionalism. But these are really the devil's bargain we make to maintain our privileged position in exchange for supporting the status quo. We confuse these with fairness, transparency, competence, moral clarity, and authenticity, which is what the people we work with are most likely to want from us. By substituting neutrality for a commitment to promoting justice and equality, we fall into the neutrality trap.

For conflict intervention practitioners in particular, neutrality and impartiality have become wrapped up in our professional identity and central to our business model. But we are not alone. Journalists, lawyers, academics, mental health professionals, teachers, physicians, and many others have made their own version of this bargain. While there is a wide array of ways we put this into practice (or choose not to), the collective impact plays a significant role in impeding social change.

On a personal level, most of us value being open-minded and recognizing the humanity in all people. But these values can suggest that everyone's grievance and narrative have equal truth and validity. If that is true, can we be truly powerful and even fierce in demanding an end to systems of oppression that privilege people who are White, male, straight, cisgender, and native-born? There is tension between our most humane instincts toward people and our commitment to challenging systems of power. Retreating to a commitment to be open-minded, impartial, and unbiased does not resolve this tension—it avoids it. And yet these values represent something important about who we are. The challenge we face is how to reconcile the seemingly contradictory pulls toward open mindedness and a commitment to social change.

This raises other important questions as well.

- Why does presenting ourselves to the world as open-minded and balanced seem so attractive?

- How does this affect our social change efforts?

- What are the forces that keep us in this particular box and how can we step out of it?

- What would our work as professionals look like without relying on the cloak of objectivity?

- When ought we to share our views and when ought we to focus on empowering others to do so?

- How can a neutral stance help us as participants in social change efforts?

- How about our day-to-day interactions with people who do not share our values or commitments but who are part of our community or workplace?

- How do we go about trying to understand what motivates those who are acting in a way that we find abhorrent?

Neutrality, Impartiality, and Objectivity

How many times have mediators and facilitators asserted that when we bring people in conflict together, we are doing so "without taking sides," that our sole purpose is to foster a constructive conversation, to clarify differences and to see if there is common ground that people might want to pursue? Even if we do not see our role as purely communication and process oriented—that is, if we identify ourselves as advocates or experts—we still profess a certain distance from the fray in the name of professionalism or objectivity. Every time we do this, we are empowering some and disempowering others—we are having an impact on the outcome and the power relations in the room.

When we try to break down our thinking about what we mean by neutrality, impartiality, and objectivity, we almost always find that we are offering something that is really impossible and that presents a false promise of safety.

Neutrality can mean:

- I have no stake in the outcome;

- I have no compromising connection with either side;

- I have no strong opinions about what should happen (or if I do, I will carefully hide these and will not let them have any impact on what I do or say);

- I am not emotionally attached to one party or set of ideas over the other;

- I will not take sides in this conflict.

But it can also mean:

- I am stuck in the middle (going neither forward nor backward—as a car in neutral);

- I don't care;

- I am not going to play a meaningful role in this interchange;

- All points of view are equally valid (even the racist ones).

Impartiality can mean:

- I am focused on process not outcome;

- Whatever outcome a group achieves is fine as long as the group genuinely embraces it;

- My behavior will not promote one side's position or the other's;

- My feelings about the issues, groups, or individuals involved will not affect my actions or recommendations.

But it can also mean:

- I don't have any particular feelings about the issues or those involved (or in the multi-partial formulation—I have feelings for everyone and every side, so it all sort of balances out);

- I don't really care about what happens;

- I can hide my feelings extremely well;

- All behavior, beliefs, and feelings are equally valid (except mine, which don't count).

Objectivity can mean:

- I can be entirely logical about an issue or dispute without letting my feelings or personal views interfere;

- I can separate facts from emotions (and people from the problem);

- I have the training, experience, and intellectual capacity to provide a dispassionate analysis.

But it can also mean:

- I don't believe morality or emotions count;

- There is a logical solution to all problems—or at least to the ones we are considering;

- "Just the facts, ma'am";

- Logic and emotions can be separated, and logic is better;

- I'm pretty smart.

Okay, maybe this is overly simplistic, but our attachment to these concepts reflects something important about how we approach conflict. And it is a problem. Any time we enter a dispute with a commitment to being neutral, impartial, and objective, we are offering something that is not credible and promoting an existing power differential. Cultures (and genders) that value objectivity and logic over passion and intuition have a built-in advantage when the processes they are engaged in are embedded in these values. We also undercut our own power when we commit to neutrality, impartiality, and objectivity by making it impossible for us to bring our whole selves to an interaction.

Clearly, these are three closely related concepts. While some have argued for offering impartiality as opposed to neutrality, the distinction between them quickly breaks down in practice. Both concepts imply a capacity to be objective, whereas objectivity implies a commitment to some level of neutrality or impartiality. ("I promise to deliver the truth even if it doesn't support our position.") These commitments are particularly concerning because they can easily reinforce oppressive social orders.

We are never truly neutral in any but an aspirational sense. That is, we can aspire to have no influence on the outcome and to avoid taking sides in any way—it is just not something that we can truly deliver. Objectivity can only be understood as one component of how we think, of how we understand the world, one which never operates in isolation of our worldview, our emotions, or our values.

When we are talking about issues where fundamental values are at stake, where power, privilege, and oppression are core concerns, and where social change is sought, a neutral or impartial stance is rightly viewed with suspicion. In these circumstances, even aspiring to be neutral or impartial is problematic. In her classic work on justice and difference, political philosopher Iris Marion Young suggested that fairness derives from heterogeneity and discourse, not impartiality:

> "Not only is impartiality impossible, however, but commitment to the ideal has adverse ideological consequences. . . . It legitimates bureaucratic authority and hierarchical decision-making processes, defusing calls for democratic decision making. And . . . it reinforces oppression by hypostatizing the point of view of privileged groups into a universal position. Instead of impartiality, I argue, we should seek public fairness, in a context of heterogeneity and partial discourse."
> (Young, *Justice and the Politics of Difference* [Princeton: Princeton University Press, 2011], 112)

If Not Neutrality, Then What?

None of this should suggest that we never focus our efforts on helping others understand and work through a conflict for themselves. Much of what underlies the commitments that interveners so often make to neutrality, impartiality, or objectivity can contribute to social change efforts. These underlying elements include:

- *Self knowledge*: It is hard to tell when our own biases are interfering with our ability to help others deal with their disputes if we don't know what those biases are.

- *Humility*: We should never assume we know better than others about what they need, what is important, what is wise. If having a background as conflict interveners has taught us anything, it is to trust that people know what they need and why.

- *Transparency:* We need to be transparent about our role, values, commitment, limits, and affiliations. People don't necessarily expect advocates and interveners to be blank slates with no beliefs or values relevant to their situation—in fact they seldom want that. But they don't want us to be coy or surreptitious about those either.

- *Authenticity:* Honesty, emotional presence, and genuine caring about the people and issues (which is often quite the opposite of what we associate with impartiality or neutrality) is central to what we have to offer.

- *Integrity:* We don't manipulate, lie, suppress narratives, disappear when the going gets rough, or pretend we are something other than what we are. We remain true to our foundational values.

- *Expertise:* We bring knowledge and experience to the table—and if we don't have in-depth technical or historical knowledge specific to a situation, we still bring more general skills in organizing, advocating, communicating, and problem-solving that are of value.

- *Respect:* We have respect for the people we are working with, for their capacity, background, and rights.

- *Courage:* We often have to deliver difficult messages, take unpopular stands, and sometimes put ourselves in harm's way if we are to play a meaningful role in conflict and social struggles.

- *Commitment to communication:* This does not mean that bringing people together to talk always makes sense, but it does mean that part of being effective in raising conflict, engaging with it in a productive way, and working across our differences requires effective communication. This is important both to how we communicate and how we help others communicate.

- *Attention to power dynamics*: Social conflict is always in part about power. When we default to an assumption that dialogue is necessary and impartiality essential, we are prone to overlook or minimize the significant power differentials involved and the way these might hijack a well-intentioned effort.

- *Independence*: We are acting according to our own values, judgment, and knowledge and not under the authority or control of others.

The Transparency Challenge

Exactly how we bring these elements to bear depends on our role and the circumstances we are in. If we are a participant in a struggle, for example, transparency about our beliefs and values will look very different than if we are a third party or professional advocate. But even as third-party interveners, the neutral stance is limiting and not nearly as effective or central to what we do as our marketing strategies and training have suggested.

When Neutrality Felt Harmful

Bernie: We have been asked to convey to you what the management is willing to do.

Protest spokesperson 1: We are all ears.

Bernie: They wish to acknowledge the concerns you have and promise to take them into consideration in their planning.

Spokesperson 2: Is that all?!

Bernie: I am afraid so. I know this is a disappointment.

Spokesperson 1: I am out of here. (She runs away–quickly and literally; this took place outside.)

Spokesperson 2: This is so full of shit. We came in good faith because we were led to expect they were ready to deal. How could you let this happen?

Bernie: I thought we were in a different place, too. I understand your anger and disappointment and wish I had different news to deliver. I will be happy to convey a response or to arrange for you to talk to a representative of management if you would like.

Spokesperson 2: We have nothing to say to them. We will respond at a time and in a manner of our own choosing.

This interchange took place during a mediation I (Bernie) conducted with a colleague between protestors engaged in peaceful civil disobedience to try to prevent the destruction of a natural area for developmental purposes and the organization overseeing the development.

We had been led to believe that some concessions from the corporate leadership would be forthcoming, perhaps procedural in nature (e.g. a commitment to negotiate an open-space plan to compensate for what would be lost in the development). But in the end the management said the most they would do is acknowledge the protesters' concerns.

I felt limited by my commitment to being impartial. What I wanted to say was, "Yes, you were played, so were we, and I am very sorry to have been part of putting you in the situation you are now in." Both my co-mediator and I felt that we couldn't truly express what we felt without violating the terms of our involvement in this conflict. But why couldn't we have said this? It was true. It might have helped them process the experience. It would not have been unfaithful to our commitment to helping promote constructive communication about the parties' essential concerns. I certainly wanted to say something that went beyond "I understand how you feel" and that acknowledged the misuse of power that had taken place. Doing so might have opened the door to more communication. But despite having written previously about the shortcomings of a neutral role, I felt stuck in it.

When Interveners' Thoughts Were Irrelevant

On the other hand, sometimes, maintaining a poker face may be important, not necessarily because it is essential to our role as interveners but because it keeps the focus of communication where it needs to be—on the parties.

"So what do you really think about wolf control?" a government official who had helped organize the Alaska Wolf Summit in early 1993 asked me (Bernie) after it was over. In fact he asked me this as Chris Moore and I were being driven to the airport on our way home to Colorado. Chris and I had just finished facilitating this week-long effort to deal with one of Alaska's most enduring controversies.

"Can't you tell?" I responded.

"Not really."

"Good!"

And with that we took our leave of this rather amazing experience, which involved about 300 invited participants and 1500 observers. The participants represented a wide spectrum of views, backgrounds, and positions and came from across the United States and Canada.

Wolf management policies in Alaska are extremely controversial and deeply ingrained in values, cultural practices, and the Alaskan identity. When Alaska elected Wally Hickel as governor, he promised to turn Alaska into a "hunter's paradise" in part by allowing for a significant cull of wolves to increase the population of caribou and moose. This led to a national boycott of Alaska by animal rights and environmental groups. Hickel responded to this by calling for a wide-ranging summit on the issues involved.

Despite the circus-like atmosphere, we felt this had been a successful effort at getting people to talk about their differences, passionately, emotionally, sometimes with anger, but often with empathy, clarity, and humor. That not much was resolved seemed beside the point. Somehow the Alaska government found a way of retreating from its most aggressive wolf control plans, the boycott

ended, and the policy-making process continues to muddle along
to this day.

It's not so much that we acted out some version of neutrality that
was key here. It's that our views were unimportant. The power relationships were not exploitative but distributive. Almost everyone
there knew more about the issues than Chris or I did. What they
needed from us was to (very) quickly create a process that would
allow for a modicum of constructive and forthright exchange.

Sometimes, the most important task for conflict interveners is
to remain focused on process and to retain credibility with parties from across a spectrum of viewpoints. I doubt anyone thought
we were completely neutral. We came from Boulder, Colorado, a
notably liberal milieu, and worked in a peacemaking profession. I
don't think anyone really cared what our personal views were. But
what people did want to make sure of was that we did not purposely
slant the process and that we provided a meaningful opportunity
for everyone to express their views. Keeping our personal views to
ourselves is a conscious strategic decision, and it is not the same as
being trapped in a neutral stance.

Activists or Professionals

Approaching social change as activists encourages a very different
way of thinking and poses different challenges than when we are
acting as professionals. These are sometimes the mirror image of
each other. As activists, we are inclined to see ourselves as all in
on one side of a controversy, conflict, or issue. As professionals (at
least in the United States and Canada), we tend to believe we have
to be objective, unbiased, and rational. Our emotions are usually
seen as impediments to our professional role. But in neither role are
these limitations necessary or helpful.

When I (Jackie) lived in Puerto Rico and provided mediation
services, the beliefs of my potential client about what made me a
credible intervener would influence whether they hired me or not.

A major global company would fly me from Puerto Rico to Florida for "delicate" cases because I was an outsider and thus could be neutral, objective, and therefore professional. In Puerto Rico, it was the other way around. I was seen as a useful and competent professional because I was an insider who could emotionally connect with them.

For some activists, being all in can suggest abandoning the strategic and empowering tool of understanding where adversaries are coming from—how they think, what they value, what pushes their buttons, what might speak to them, and the narratives they tell that support their thinking and guide their strategies.

Activists need to maintain their passion as they pursue their strategies for change. But if as activists we cannot sometimes step back and try to understand how others are thinking (not what we think of their thinking—but what they actually think and why), including what they believe about us, then we are giving up a major strategic asset. Helping activists to think about this is one way conflict specialists can sometimes provide a useful service to advocates.

As professionals, we need to use our full array of analytic and strategic tools to understand the essence of our role. But our values, passions, commitments, and narratives are also important. Without them we can't fully engage and connect with others, and our services are not going to be as effective. When we are in a client role, we can readily experience this. For example, as clients, we want our therapists to genuinely care about us, to like us, to be committed to us, and to respect us—even as we write the check. We may want them to take our side in a marital dispute even though we may know they won't, and we want them to see when we are being reasonable (in our own view) and when our spouse is not (again in our own view). We want our lawyers not just to represent us but to believe in us. We want our mediators to get where we are coming from and to recognize when we are not being treated well.

What do we want our therapist/lawyer/mediator to do if they don't think we are behaving reasonably or in the right? Do we want them to suppress their views or to share them? We suspect that most often, we would rather know what our trusted advisers think, even though we may not always react well. But we don't want to be put into a corner or disempowered, either. We want respect but honesty, fairness but support, authenticity but keeping a focus on our needs. Not an easy row to hoe as professionals but an essential one. And neutrality in this sense is just avoidance.

The Many Faces of the Neutrality Trap: Fairness and False Equivalence

How do journalists report the views and concerns of conspiracy theorists, anti-Semites, and racists in an evenhanded manner without falling into the trap of false equivalence (assuming all points of view are equally valid—"everyone has a right to their opinion")? How should legitimate news organizations cover Big Lies (such as "I won this election in a landslide") without either identifying it as a lie or giving it undue credence or airtime? For that matter, how can any of us try to understand the sources of racism and fascism in this era without simultaneously condemning the views and actions of QAnon adherents or Proud Boys?

We can't. And we shouldn't. It's an unfair challenge and forces us to play the equivalence game. And it truly is false equivalence. Whether we are journalists, students of conflict, political scientists, or judges, none of us comes to this as a blank slate, and no one expects us to. Our beliefs are part of what we bring to the table. But that does not mean we can't allow QAnon believers to have a voice. It's just that we have an obligation to put that voice in perspective. That is to say—we need to point out that almost all of what they say is dangerous and nonsensical, but that nonetheless they are having an impact on our world, so we better understand it. Part of understanding is trying to get inside their thinking and their life experience, which naturally includes some genuine concerns. But we ought not fall into the *false equivalence fallacy*. Just because there are different points of view does not mean they are all reasonable. Trying to understand each point of view does not mean we have to treat them as equally valid—or valid at all.

Watching journalists struggle with this dilemma is at times painful. Some don't even really try. They are journalists or analysts in name only—and it would be better for them to give up that title and accept that they are propagandists and entertainers. Sometimes, in the name of fairness, they conduct dueling narrative panels, cloaked as analyses from different points of view. And sometimes they dissolve into a kind of "he said, she said" presentation. Which is more problematic, a false pretense of objectivity or the outrage or disdain that conscientious journalists sometimes express? As an example, Anderson Cooper of CNN commented about a ranting Donald Trump, the day after he lost the election: "That is the president of the United States. That is the most powerful person in the world. We see him like an obese turtle on his back flailing in the hot sun, realizing his time is over." He later apologized for not acting in accordance with his values, although his honesty was refreshing (Matthews 2020).

Manifestations of false equivalence are everywhere, and a common mechanism for dismissing the danger of extremism (particularly of the right-wing kind) is the use of "whataboutsim." For example:

"What about the violence at Black Lives Matter rallies?"

"What about the extremism of the Antifas?"

"Why are Democrats so quick to criticize QAnon supporters when they promote their own conspiracy theories about Trump, such as in the Steele Report?"

Does being fair and open-minded mean that we need to treat these obviously extremely different phenomena (e.g. organized, armed militias storming the Michigan and federal capitols, and some occasional looting and vandalism on the periphery of BLM movements) as equivalent? How can we adhere to a principled approach to fighting for social change without accepting the right of others to fight against what they see as a fraudulent election?

There is no easy way through this dilemma. We want the news to be fair, but we don't want to substitute phony objectivity for presenting what is really happening. We don't want to present lies as if they might be true, but it's also a bit annoying to read or hear caveats inserted into every story indicating that a statement is untrue, unproven, or more simply a lie. Is it better to routinely repeat the caveats or just let the statement stand?

In the end, what we most likely want of journalists is similar to what we want of mediators: authenticity, transparency, integrity, and honesty. Part of the honesty we want is about the ideas and beliefs of the reporter or analyst, but we also don't want this to take over the story they are presenting. We also want emotional honesty. A journalist who is having a genuine emotional reaction to a story they are reporting and who is willing to share it can help bring a story to life—emotions are part of the picture. But we also want to be left the space to have our own reactions and come to our own conclusions.

This presents a difficult challenge but not an impossible one. David Begnaud, a CBS reporter who covered Hurricane María in Puerto Rico in 2017, provided an excellent example of emotional authenticity in reporting. In an interview with CBS, he shared how he made the decision to assert his own humanity and allow his heart to enter into his reporting:

> "This whole idea of what I am supposed to do or what I am not supposed to do—listen, at CBS we have ethics, we have standards that we follow . . . But at the end of the day, we are humans and I've got a heart too. And I followed that. And what that meant was that . . . I thought the most adequate way of covering it was living it. [. . .] I just wanted to be where they were. Because that was the most honest way of making you feel what they were feeling"
> (Begnaud, "David Begnaud reflects on Hurricane Maria coverage," CBS News, YouTube, June 9, 2018)

Begnaud avoided the neutrality trap by being authentic, embracing emotion, and using the power of naming without focusing on "fixing" the situation. As the interview illustrates, Begnaud honored his values and acknowledged the power differential between the colony and the empire.

We also want to be fair and open-minded in our own lives, and it can be confusing to navigate the competing values and realities at play here. These three underlying principles are critical, if difficult to apply:

- We should always respect the right of all people to advocate for their essential interests in a nonviolent way.

- We should never lose sight of our own basic values.

- We should pay attention to issues of privilege and power that are in essence why these equivalences are false.

Power and Neutrality

For a negotiation or dialogue to have integrity and to be fair, power differences must be taken into account. These are embedded in the structure of the institutions and culture where the interaction is located. Of particular importance are structural power differentials based on race, culture, gender, and class. We discuss these throughout this book, but let's take a brief look at them here, using an example from the child welfare system.

Consider a single parent who has been reported to a child protection agency for neglect due to substance abuse. This parent is about to encounter a system that is functioning under a rather rigid set of laws that are in theory designed to protect children but also support parents and families. The process of decision making will be governed by supposedly objective criteria, fact-based assessments, and rational consideration of highly emotional and stressful challenges. The professionals who have worked in this system over a period of time are likely to know each other and to have developed a set of attitudes about what works, what children need, and how likely it is for parents to overcome these types of problems. They may be able to empathize with the parent's situation, or they may be too burned out or jaded to do so except in a performative manner. Regardless, the procedures they follow assume that the decision-making process will be balanced, objective, and conducted in an impartial manner. But almost inevitably it won't. Communication norms, for example, are likely to make the sharing of any anger, desperation, or depression on the part of the parent as a sign of incapacity to parent, denial of the problem, or resistance to change. Even professionals who are assigned to be advocates for the parent are likely to do all they can to mold the discussion in the professional mode of discourse and to place the parent in the role of the supplicant.

If the parent participates in a dialogue process, for example, family group decision making or child protection mediation, the very commitment a facilitator or mediator makes to neutrality can easily further disempower the parent who is in an alienating setting to begin with. To accomplish anything like a fair process, the intervener will almost certainly have to find a way to enhance the parent's power and to address the structural imbalances built into the process (Mayer 2009).

Now consider how the power dynamics are likely to be affected if the parent is from a different culture, race, class, or all three. What if they don't speak the same language, are of a different age, or if gender identification is raised as an issue? In this setting some differences of this nature are very likely. The role of the extended family and the village, different norms about discipline, how one is expected to talk to people in authority, how (or whether) to share emotions, and how to talk about deeply personal and perhaps embarrassing issues are likely to be sources not just of differences but of incomprehensibility. To approach a situation like this with a commitment to encouraging a frank and productive conversation in fact requires that we abandon, or at least significantly modify, what we might ordinarily consider to be a neutral, impartial, objective, fact-based approach.

Dealing with family norms and child rearing as professionals or advocates is an arena in which the problem with neutrality is stark and readily understandable. But we can see similar dynamics in workplaces, healthcare, criminal justice, education, police-community interactions, and environmental decision making. The challenge for professionals is to understand the critical importance of moving outside the protective envelope of professional distance while maintaining the perspective and the analytical tools that are essential to their role and contribution. The challenge for activists is to utilize the perspective and knowledge that professionals have without buying into the mystique of objectivity and impartiality that professionals so often promote.

This is no small challenge, and it infuses a plethora of interactions across our society. But if we are to work toward a sustainable effort at social change, the neutrality trap has to be confronted.

Reflective Dialogue: Neutrality

Bernie: Jackie, earlier in this chapter I shared a time when I thought being in a neutral role felt like I was contributing to an unjust outcome or at least interaction. Have you ever felt that way?

Jackie: Yes, especially in the early stages of my career as a mediator. As you know, I was a litigating lawyer before becoming a mediator. Therefore, the idea of remaining silent

(Continued)

(Continued)

under the pretense of needing to be neutral has always been a struggle for me. I clearly remember one of my first mediations at the Equal Employment Opportunity Commission (EEOC) in which the employee/complainant had an incompetent lawyer. During the process of drafting the agreement it became clear that the attorney was providing legal advice that would result in his client unknowingly signing an agreement that was not in the client's best interest. As a mediator, I tried just about everything short of providing legal advice to let the employee's attorney and his client know that they needed to carefully read the latest regulations regarding the matter that was being addressed. At the end, luckily for everyone, the agency's attorney decided to share the information regarding the latest regulation and point-blank told the employee's attorney that what he was proposing was in detriment to his client. He not only asked for a break so he could print the regulations but also proceeded to interpret them for the employee and his attorney. I later asked the agency's attorney why he had intervened, and he said that he was more concerned about justice being done for the employee than having a "win." At the time, I felt trapped by the notion of remaining neutral and the principle that I could not use my legal knowledge because as a mediator I was in a "neutral role." I decided that I would never let neutrality cause a travesty of justice. It also led me to reflect on my moral obligation about what I hear in a "neutral space." If we are to go beyond reaching individual agreements and actually change unjust social systems, what do we do with what we hear? Bernie, how did you arrive at your current views about neutrality?

Bernie: A teacher I formerly worked with used to say, "Never let your values get in the way of doing what's right."

The Neutrality Trap   49

That is how I have often felt about neutrality. The neutrality-impartiality-objectivity stance that frames so much of how we try to report the news, analyze conflicts, and solve problems has bothered me from the beginning of my work as a conflict intervener. Early on, being neutral seemed like a key part of our identity and our business model. It also played into my own conflict-avoidant tendencies. But the longer I worked as a third party, the more this stance seemed morally compromising, intellectually suspect, and unnecessary. I have gone through successive stages of distancing myself from this. I began to realize that what I did in practice, what I taught, and what I really believed were out of sync with each other, and my struggle with coming to terms with this over the years has been reflected in my writing (see Mayer 2004, 2011, 2015, 2018). Among the most frequent—and affirming—responses to these have been the many expressions of appreciation that I received from colleagues for articulating their often-inchoate discomfort with neutrality. The tension in aligning our commitment to speaking out against injustice and our desire to be fair and open-minded is widespread—and essential to building effective social movements.

Why do you think neutrality has become such a central component in the identity of conflict specialists and so many other professions?

Jackie: Historically, neutrality has been a way for professions to preserve the status quo and sustain oppressive structures. If you remain neutral, you preserve the existing social order and its inequities. This works well for the dominant group in any society or institution. In the case of conflict specialists, many of the conflict models and processes focus on problem solving and advancing social justice within the

(Continued)

(*Continued*)

confines of the dominant social norms. Many "neutrals" are eager to assist conflicting parties in navigating structures of oppressions but not to change the structures in significant ways. As a Puerto Rican woman who has worked in professions traditionally reserved for White men, I have often experienced the injustices of neutrality. Being neutral becomes an excuse for ensuring that an individual conflict is addressed (sometimes), but not the system and the structures that caused the conflict in the first place. For example, this can take place when a mediator tells a party to focus solely on his/her issue and not what affects other individuals outside the mediation. It is a way of unintentionally (or intentionally) fragmenting a conflict that is nested in unjust social or institutional structures. However, professions don't frame this behavior as fragmenting or ignoring but rather as being objective and professional. If we truly want to advance social movements, disrupt oppressive systems, transform institutions, and build more just structures, we must avoid falling in the neutrality trap.

chapter three

intersectionality and social change

"There is no such thing as a single-issue struggle because we do not live single-issue lives"

—Audre Lorde, "Learning from the '60s"

All of us approach the conflicts in our lives and the social activ-ism we engage in with both privilege and vulnerabilities. Understanding this is essential to our efforts at both constructive conflict engagement and system change. This requires delving into our own intersectional identity and into the pervasive role of race, gender, and intersectionality in everything we do. Who are we? What are we drawn to? What are our experiences with privilege or the lack thereof? We therefore start this chapter with a reflection on our own intersectionality.

Understanding Our Intersectionality

Jackie: "Don't cross Cummings! It's dangerous there." That implied (and sometimes spoken) admonition was clear and present at Creighton University, the primarily White institution where we both worked. What was on the other side of the street? North Omaha—Omaha's predominantly African American community.

It turned out that from the standpoint of many of my White colleagues, I should also avoid going to South Omaha, located about 10 miles from Creighton, especially at nights. Historically, South Omaha was known as an immigrant area. In the 1800s many European immigrants came to work in the stockyards and meat-packing centers. Nowadays the majority of the Hispanic population in South Omaha are Mexicans.

The emphasis on "especially at nights" had to do with being a woman. Simultaneously, my Latinx friends were warning me not to hang a crucifix on the rear window of my car because it could be dangerous, especially if driving near South Omaha. For many Omaha police officers, a crucifix in the rear window served as a marker of Latinx identity, and anyone displaying it could be identified as such and could expect harassment and abuse.

Warnings (myths) of this nature are prevalent across Canada and the United States, and they are damaging. They perpetuate the implicit biases that pervade our institutions and interfere with our capacity for turning our differences into a source of strength and a resource to advance social justice (Young 2000). If we are not part of the social network of our neighboring African American community, we will not understand the impact our experience of privilege has on their experience of racism. We cannot bring about social change if we cannot share our stories across the boundaries of privilege and race.

These various warnings reflected my intersectional identity. Some of my colleagues were seeing me as White and as a woman. My Latinx friends were seeing me as a Puerto Rican woman from the Caribbean who spoke with an accent (my native language is Spanish). My whiteness provided certain privileges with my White colleagues that my Black or darker-skinned friends did not have, including concern for my physical safety. However, at the intersection of my whiteness and Caribbean identity, my whiteness started to wane and with it my privilege. My relocation from Puerto Rico to Omaha highlighted my Caribbean otherness. I went from dealing with the challenges of being a woman in a straight male–dominated world to the complexity of bigotry and privilege at the intersection of race, national origin, and gender.

I have experienced these patterns of intersectionality in many work settings in the United States. In part because of my more privileged position in Puerto Rico (as White and middle class), it took me some time to be able to name this. Was the person refusing to pack my bags (and only mine) at a supermarket because I was with my Black Puerto Rican friend or because they were tired? Did a waitress neglect to serve our table because she did not see us or because we were speaking in Spanish? Yes, I was closer to the spectrum of whiteness than my Black friends, but not close enough to enjoy all the privileges.

Bernie: I come from both a privileged and a vulnerable background. I am an older White male, and while my family was not wealthy (my parents were social workers), they were able to support me through my years in college. But I am also Jewish, the child of Holocaust survivors (my father survived the Buchenwald concentration camp—barely, my mother's parents did not survive), and I am now a senior citizen (75 at the time of this writing). I am also straight and cisgender.

For most of my life, my privilege has predominated, but not always. I have been subjected to my fair share of anti-Semitic remarks or slights. For example:

- Multiple incidents of having to deal with anti-Semitic tropes about Jews and money ("They were trying to 'Jew down' the price." "You should be our treasurer; I am sure you are good at managing money.").

- "This high school has too many Jews to produce a good football team." (An English teacher.)

- "What does the Jewish professor have to say about baseball?" (30 years before I was actually a professor—we were just talking about sports.)

- A "stone soap" (reference to Nazi extermination camps)
  joke from a drunk board member of an organization where
  I worked and the failure of leadership to do anything when
  I complained.

Most of these were annoying primarily because I felt caught
between whether to confront the behavior or let it go, and this
created internal tension for me about my identity. Was I going to
go "all Jewish," call out the behavior and spend the time and emotional energy required to deal with it? Was I going to go along as
another one of the (White, male) gang and respond with humor or
avoidance? Or was I going to try to find a way to do both? I have
tried all the above. None works perfectly, but letting it go entirely
makes me feel terrible. Confronting it in a way that invites further conversation has sometimes opened a stronger relationship,
but at other times it has just led to awkward silences, superficial
responses, or quick changes of the subject.

Several incidents stand out as more painful examples of bigotry.
These leave a lasting impression. For example, when I was about 9,
my parents (who had thick German accents, which I never heard
as such) and I were looking for a motel while on a road trip. We
passed quite a few "No Vacancy" signs but eventually there was
a fairly large facility with a brightly lit vacancy light. When we
tried to book a room, however, we were told that they were full.
My father pointed out that their sign indicated otherwise, but the
manager said all that they had left was a dormitory style room for
twelve. My dad said we would take it. We were refused. He was
angry, my mother sad, and I was confused. Were we turned away
because of being Jewish, because my parents were clearly immigrants, because they were German? Who knows? Does it matter?
One way or another it was an act of oppression.

Sometimes unwillingness to engage is almost as bad as overt
bigotry. When *Schindler's List* came out, well after my father's death,

my mother insisted on seeing it. It was painful for her to view, but she felt that "never again" meant we had to "keep telling the story." My mother found it very hard to talk about the Holocaust, and while my father was alive, she deferred to him to relate what they had experienced. But after he died, she felt it was her obligation to continue to tell their story. And so she forced herself to speak about it, often in very public venues. In contrast, several friends chose not to see *Schindler's List* because "it was just too painful for them to watch all that suffering."

Not infrequently, I hear similar statements made about other movies, TV shows, or documentaries that deal with the Holocaust, slavery, genocide, or other horrendous experiences. Inevitably, I think of my mother's courage and feel that if she could watch *Schindler's List*, we can watch *Small Axe*, *The Underground Railroad*, or *The Hunting Ground* (to take some recent examples), and we can talk about it. I find it remarkable that in writing this, all sorts of additional memories of anti-Semitism are surfacing—and I feel angry.

But to reiterate, for the most part I have been privileged, and as I have grown older, I am even sometimes treated with respect for these past experiences that have formed my identity. Sometimes, being the son of Holocaust survivors has opened the door to interesting, important, and deepening conversations. And as an older White guy, I have been able to stand up to casual racist remarks and with people who were being subjected to bigotry. At times Jackie and I have been allies in our efforts to deal with hostile working environments; I have felt Jackie has had my back, and I believe I have had hers.

Occasionally, it was the very intersectional nature of my identity that allowed me to be an ally. I could speak with a certain authenticity because of my familiarity with the trauma that went along with being a Holocaust survivor and yet from the relatively secure position of being a White man with certain status and privilege.

Intersectionality and Oppression

The concept of *intersectionality* was coined by Kimberlé Crenshaw (1989), a legal scholar. Crenshaw critiqued the fragmented manner in which the courts interpreted discrimination cases brought by African American women. *DeGraffenreid v. General Motors* (ED Mo 1976) illustrates her point. Emma DeGraffenreid, an African American woman, alleged that the company's seniority policy discriminated against Black women. General Motors did not hire Black women prior to 1964. Therefore, when the company implemented seniority-based layoff policies, they terminated the contracts of all their Black female employees. The court dismissed her case on the grounds that the company hired African Americans (mostly men for maintenance jobs) and women (mostly White to do clerical jobs).

Crenshaw (1989) argued that framing the experiences of African American women as either exclusively Black or exclusively female created modes of discrimination that left them without a legal remedy. Their experiences needed to be considered in a wholistic manner; they were both Black and women. The source of their oppression was the result of the intersection of gender and race, which generated unique challenges. The court's narrow view of discrimination perpetuated racism by ignoring the company's history of refusing to hire Black women not because they were Black or female but because they were both.

My (Jackie's) experience with seniority policies is that minoritized groups are always at a disadvantage and are usually the first to go. In a society with a long history of discrimination, any policy that uses seniority as a sole or essential criterion will most likely be inequitable.

Crenshaw named an experience that was well known to women of color and lesbians who had joined the feminist movements of the 1970s and 1980s (Atewologun 2018). Many of these women felt that White women advanced their own liberation cause while ignoring the impact that race, sexual preference, class, and age had on their unique experiences of oppression. In Lorde's (2017, 96) words, "There is a pretense to a homogeneity of experience covered by the word *sisterhood* that does not in fact exist." In other words, White, middle-class women with heterosexual orientation often did not recognize how multiple forces of oppression were fused together for other women. Black women in turn did not always recognize that White women's experiences are not all the same.

The dynamics of intersectionality have profound implications for how we engage with conflict at the individual and systemic level. How do we organize across differences to bring about social change? How can intersectionality expose interconnections of oppressive power structures? How can we bring together and keep diverse people united as they work toward a common goal? When we join a social movement, we bring with us our diverse identities and our multiple ways of making meaning and experiencing events.

We need to recognize the implications of this for how we see others and they see us. This starts with understanding that we can't ever fully understand what someone else has been through nor can they fully understand our experiences. The more we can listen to each other, share our experiences and our power, and create an atmosphere in which it's safe to raise difficult issues, the more effective our efforts at building a movement and dealing with enduring conflicts will be.

In her recent book, *The Purpose of Power*, Alicia Garza (2020) writes that in social movements and in coalitions of diverse groups, there is a tendency to shut down someone who names a situation or behavior that is uncomfortable. The reason often given for this is that everyone needs to be nice to each other and to focus on working toward common goals. Although we should not lose sight of these goals, shutting down these types of conversations prevents us from building the relationships across differences that can empower social movements.

The groups that we have been involved with that seemed to us to be most able to engage in a deep and meaningful way about difficult issues appeared to share three characteristics:

- They were diverse;

- Group norms supported raising difficult issues; and

- Group members took time to get to know each other and their circumstances.

Even though people sometimes delivered hard messages, they were mostly able to talk through their differences and continue to work toward a common goal. Sometimes these differences and the conversations about them forged a new level of connection. The group's cohesiveness and resiliency were then strengthened, and as a result they were better able to withstand the pushback and divisive tactics that they inevitably faced when their purpose was to change the status quo in some way.

Cohesion is especially important in the face of divisive tactics that are often used to split those fighting against racist systems. One particularly disturbing example of this has been the way lightness has been used as a hierarchical standard (Kendi 2019). The closer we are to being white, the less oppression we will experience and the more privilege we will have. Paradoxically, if we occupy the space at the intersection of whiteness and a minoritized group (e.g. White Latina), the more invisible racial oppression becomes and the less empathy and support victims are likely to receive. As a White Latina, I (Jackie) have often experienced this particular complexity of intersectionality, especially when I have relocated from Puerto Rico to the United States to study or work.

Of course, as individuals and groups we are far from perfect in accomplishing this level of cohesion. We sometimes avoid difficult issues, frame our concerns in divisive or damaging ways, and are not the best listeners. Sometimes we go for superficial resolution of issues that run deep and repress our own feelings and biases to the point that we don't recognize them. In other words, we are human, and the groups we belong to are imperfect as well. But the more we work to nurture relationships across our differences and the more we are able as a group to create an atmosphere that allows for difficult conversations to happen, the more able we will be to become a force for effective action.

Intersectionality creates unique challenges and opportunities for transformation. Challenges because it is difficult to see the multiple forces of oppressions that some are subjected to. When we fail to see these intersections, we risk prioritizing one type of oppression over another and even discounting the pain and suffering of another human being. But our intersectionality is also a source of connection that can help us to build alliances across the spectrum of oppression. This can be a transformational experience that greatly enhances the power of our social change efforts.

Challenging the Marginalization of the "Other"

Social movements give voice to groups who do not fit in as equals and are labeled as different, deviant, and not deserving of the same social benefits and legal protections as those in the dominant group. These non-dominant groups occupy spaces in which they are not fully recognized, legally or socially, because they fall outside of the accepted social order and are therefore viewed with disdain or dismissal (Butler 1993; Abeijon 2014). We have all seen the results of this abuse of power and of the structural violence that results. Women do not get equal pay for equal work, Black men are killed by police at a higher rate than White men, Latinxs die of COVID-19 at a higher rate than Whites, and same-sex marriage was prohibited until very recently.

Diversity enriches our experiences and creates opportunities for growth and innovation, but it presents challenges as well. Diversity increases the possibility of conflict. The clashing of worldviews and opposing interests among diverse groups is inevitable, and cohesion decreases with diversity (Putnam 2007). And yet, we also know that having diverse teams increases our capacity to solve complex problems (Page 2007).

But doing so means challenging the existing distribution of power. For those in the dominant power position, this possibility is likely to be frightening and viewed as a matter of winning or losing. When a group of students demand that the administration hire more women in tenure-track faculty positions, male faculty can feel that they are under attack, or when students and faculty demand university support for ethnic studies programs, other programs may fear a decrease in resources or students. When the competition for resources or power in any institution occurs in the context of racial or gender differences, the problem takes on a very different dimension. In that case, those in the dominant group will almost always see the redistribution of power as a zero-sum game in which they lose out, rather than a way to strengthen the entire system. Sometimes, this tension is used by those in power to keep exploited groups divided.

When I (Bernie) was 18, I worked in a factory that manufactured home repair products. My department produced packaging materials that were then used by a different department to prepare the products for shipping. I almost set off racial combat when I proposed a new way to transfer these materials that would make our operations more efficient. When we implemented this, the workers in the other department became enraged, provoking an angry counterreaction from others in my department. The management thanked me for my efforts but told me to let it go. This made no sense to me until I considered the racial dynamics. Aside from me, all those employed in my department were African American, whereas the receiving department was made up entirely of Eastern European immigrants. We should have been natural allies in a workplace that offered only minimum wage and no benefits, but management exploited racial tensions to keep us divided.

Experiencing Conflict Through Intersectionality

Demographic shifts in the United States, Canada, the United Kingdom, and elsewhere are increasing the proportion of racial minorities contributing to the complexity of the intersectionality matrix. By 2045 people of color will become a majority of the US population, and we will most likely see a dramatic increase in foreign-born Americans as well (US Census Bureau 2020, 7). This is disrupting the US national sense of identity and presenting a challenge to its legal, economic, political, educational, and healthcare systems, all of which developed in a much less diverse society.

The fear of the "other" gaining power has mobilized the privileged elite to do everything within its reach to hold on to its political power. Many US states have escalated voting suppression strategies by passing legislation that makes it harder for the emerging minority-majority to vote. According to the Brennan Center for Justice, a voting rights advocacy group, as of February 19, 2021, 253 bills that include measures restricting voting rights had been introduced into 43 state legislatures (Samuels, Mejía, and Rakich 2021).

Proposed restrictive mechanisms include requiring driver's licenses, prohibiting the distribution of water or food to people waiting in line to vote, and decreasing the time and locations for voting (Samuels, Mejía, and Rakich 2021). These restrictions disproportionately affect the poor and BIPOC (Black, Indigenous, and People of Color) communities. Studies in the United States confirm that Latinx and Black voters are already forced to wait significantly longer in lines than White voters (Klain et al. 2020; Cohen 2020, 173–182). And now, in some states, they will not be able to accept water or food while doing so.

As our societies become more diverse, we will encounter many more efforts of the dominant culture to hold on to power. Clearly, this will be a major focus of social movements in the years ahead. But we should also celebrate our diversity as a source of strength and frame the goals we are pursuing and the movements we are building in keeping with our intersectional realities.

Moving Away from a Single Story

Multilayered systems of injustice call for a response that honors each of our unique stories and for us to reject what novelist Chimamanda Ngozi Adichie has referred to as the "danger of a single story." Adichie (2009) contends that single stories are dangerous because they "rob people from their humanity" by assuming that one identity or experience represents the sole truth or point of view. When we become aware of how power is experienced and resisted at the crossroads of our identities, we can use both our differences and our similarities as a connecting force. We can frame our cause so that everyone finds their space within the movement for social change.

Vieques is a 21-by-3-miles island and Puerto Rican municipality. During the 1940s, the US Congress approved legislation to expropriate 63 to 78 percent of Vieques land forcing 40 to 50 percent of its population to relocate. The island was used by the US Navy for its war games. The Navy created dossiers with photos and fingerprints for Viequenses, which they were expected to use every time they entered or exited their own island (Font-Guzmán and Alemán 2010,135).

The US Navy put forth a racist and colonialist story about the "locals" (that is, Viequenses). Chief Anne Bradford, the Navy's public relations officer, put it this way: "They don't understand what the Navy is about. It's like a third-world country. They can't understand—it's like expounding on Newton's theory to an eighteen-month-old baby" (McCaffrey 2002, 114–116). Lieutenant Commander Tom McDonald, a government liaison officer, described Viequenses as lacking work ethic: "When you get down to it, they're lazy . . . They don't want to work. If there were industrious people here, we could do so much" (McCaffrey 2002, 114–116).

Puerto Ricans from the island and the diaspora, with differing political ideologies, religious affiliations, racial identities, and socioeconomic statuses, joined forces to demand that the US Navy leave Vieques. These diverse groups created a force for change that allowed them to connect through their similarities and differences. The conflict was shifted from a question of ownership and national defense—colonial politics as usual—to a national and international protest for social justice and peace.

The violence of the Navy against Viequenses was framed as an attack against all Puerto Ricans, and instead of fighting each other along ideological lines, they came together to assert their collective cultural and national identity (Font-Guzmán and Alemán 2010, 139). The movement allowed people to express both their unique and collective experiences of oppressions. This is one of the few times in the history of Puerto Rico that this kind of unity was achieved. Puerto Ricans were able to create a counternarrative that moved beyond a single story and was inclusive of all Puerto Ricans.

Acknowledging Pain in Ourselves and Others

"Nobody is free until everybody is free."
—*Fannie Lou Hamer*

"Your pain is the breaking of the shell that encloses your understanding."
—*Kahlil Gibran, 1960, The Prophet*

Doing the hard work of transforming spaces of oppression is painful, uncertain, and at times traumatic in ways that negatively affect health (Menakem 2017, 40). "Traumatic retention" occurs when an individual or a group of people subjected to repeated violence over time internalizes their trauma and passes it down generationally (ibid, 9). Similarly in the context of colonialism,

Sartre described the status of the oppressed as "a nervous condition" (Fanon 1963, 20).

African Americans and Indigenous populations have experienced generations of trauma after centuries of slavery and genocide. So have Puerto Ricans and those living in other colonies as a result of the long-term exploitation they have experienced. These traumas reverberate in the present every time a Black man is murdered by a White policeman or a Black woman unsuccessfully uses the legal system to seek justice as in the case of Emma DeGraffenreid or when over 1000 undocumented corpses are found in Canada on the grounds of former state-funded Christian "residential schools" that were part of a forced cultural assimilation effort of First Nations children (Blackstock 2021).

For Whom Are "Safe Spaces" Safe?

Trauma that stems from oppression is epidemic in scale and impact. We cannot just go in, fix the problem, and move on. To deal with this, we need to look to the future, but we also need to come to terms with the past. When organizations hold listening or dialogue sessions in "safe spaces" to address issues of racism and to try to become more inclusive, while appreciating the intention, we wonder, safe for whom? Are those conducting the sessions working to ensure that participants are not retraumatized?

Diversity training, sometimes delivered by conflict interveners, has a long history and is an outgrowth of corporate sensitivity training, which has been around in one form or another since the early fifties (Blum 2020). Diversity training has been criticized from both the left and the right. The Trump administration attempted to ban these trainings claiming they are divisive, anti-American, and wasteful. This was in keeping with Trump's denial of systemic racism. Others have criticized these sessions as superficial, avoiding genuine discussions of race and racism and substituting talk for action (Kendi 2019; Lasch-Quinn 2001). But even when efforts are made to enter into meaningful discussions about race, they often fail to take into account how unsafe it can feel for people to speak up.

I (Jackie) have lost count of how many times I have been told to moderate my tone, limit my story, or flat out not tell it because it may cause others to become defensive. I have been told a complaint is "under investigation," an investigation which never goes anywhere. I have often chosen to speak up, not as an act of bravery but of desperation. Sometimes the advice to remain silent from those in positions of power has come from a genuine concern for my well-being, but it has invariably been the wrong advice. What I wanted to hear was how I could be supported in raising my concerns and telling my story. How could others provide support in preempting and managing any backlash that might follow? What did I need to be safe? The decision to speak up has not readily resulted in systemic change, but it has enabled me to find allies along the way, to forge relationships and supportive networks. With the support of these newly found allies and networks, I have been able to participate in and at times lead initiatives for change.

Most of my oppressive experiences as a Puerto Rican woman in the United States have been triggered by a system's silence. Oppression often manifests itself through not acknowledging our successes or recognizing our pain and by "leaving out" part of the story. This increases the difficulty of naming the behavior because we are naming "the absence of." If we decide to name the omission, it places us in the awkward position of coming across as petty or self-centered. And yet, to truly move toward healing, we must learn how to see the unseen and hear the unspoken. As a Latina in the United States, I am often not seen or, if I am seen, not noticed. This is a common feeling for those from a nondominant group. We start seeing the structures of oppression that are hidden in plain sight. Gloria Anzaldua (1999, 60) talks about how minoritized groups develop a "facultad," which is "the capacity to see in surface phenomena the meaning of deeper realities, to see the deep structure below the surface." Once we see these structures, it is impossible to unsee them. This is one of the many reasons that sharing stories across differences is so effective. It provides an opportunity for those who are in a position of privilege to see and notice the violence. Once they see it, they are more likely to join in, making change happen.

The Challenges of Allyship

I (Bernie) have known Jordan since I was a teenager, and during my early 20s, we worked together as childcare workers at a residential treatment center in Cleveland. Jordan is about eight years older than me, an African American from a poor neighborhood in a southern city. We became good friends and remained so after I moved away from Ohio. Whenever I returned to Cleveland, Jordan and I would get together. Once, when meeting in a coffee shop in Shaker Heights, an incident occurred that I have often thought about. What most strikes me is my obliviousness to an obviously racist incident and Jordan's reticence to talk about it.

We were sitting at a table each with a cup of coffee when a White waitress came by and asked me if I wanted a refill, which I did not, so she moved on. A moment passed and Jordan said, "She never asked me." I had not even noticed (my years of activism on race and related issues notwithstanding). I was dumbfounded. I asked Jordan if he wanted me to ask her to return. He did not. Did he think this was about race? His look was a sort of mixture of "DUH!" and "I am not going there." I felt terrible but also inept. I wanted to do something. He did not. I wanted to process what had happened. He was having none of that. So our discussion moved on.

Jordan was by that time a psychotherapist and professor. Our long friendship, shared values, and supposed relationship skills made no difference. From my point of view, my failure to notice, to name, and to do something was disappointing to say the least. I felt I was being a lousy "ally." But I also felt that Jordan was in a no-win situation. If he felt we had to act so I could feel better, he would be putting himself in a position he did not feel safe in. If he talked about this, he would be accessing emotions that he was not willing to delve into at that place or with me. I know he was acutely sensitive to being seen as an angry Black man and perhaps his apprehensions about this were greater than his need to confront yet another incident of racism or to talk about it.

Incidents like this point out our blind spots and the way in which everyday incidents of racism are so common that those of us with privilege often fail to notice them. We both know from our work in conflict and from studies of how people respond to power differentials that those with more power and resources tend to be oblivious of their privilege while those with less are acutely aware of the power dynamics (Coleman 2000). Learning to be more aware and more adept at using this awareness to be good allies and partners in social change is a never-ending challenge.

Silencing someone's story (or ignoring opportunities to help them tell it) prevents healing and holds back change. Silence takes many forms, including going through the motions of listening, but whatever form it takes, it inhibits reaching out and connecting with others. If we truly want to listen, and especially if we are coming from a dominant group, we need to be willing to hear unedited, raw, and often painful stories. We especially need to listen to the parts of these stories that cause us discomfort, and in the process we need to listen to the silences as well. We need to help develop and support processes that allow everyone to share their full story in their way and at a time and space of their choosing, even as we might help create opportunities for this to happen.

The Conscious and Unconscious Bases of Racism

Racist policies, even after they are formally revoked, are sustained and replicated through individual actions in the way we engage with each other and in the social norms that we perpetuate. As conflict interveners we regularly see the lasting impact of these biases and assumptions about who holds power. This is sometimes explicit and conscious, but implicit bias is everywhere.

Our explicit biases can be extremely hurtful, but they also can be easier to deal with. For example, consider the video taken by Christian Cooper of Amy Cooper (no relationship) calling the police claiming that she was being threatened by an African American man. Cooper, a Black man, was bird-watching in New York City when he politely asked Amy Cooper, a White woman, to comply with ordinances requiring that she leash her dog in that part of Central Park. The enormous public response to this video by and large condemned Amy Cooper's behavior. But what if her bias was less overt, if it had not been filmed, or if the response of Christian Cooper had not been so calm and deliberate to both Amy Cooper and the police officer who responded to her call? The sheer clarity of her attempt to invoke White privilege made it easier to respond to for many who reject racism.

Implicit Bias and Racism

Bias is almost always at least in part unconscious. When we have prejudicial attitudes and hold stereotypes without our conscious knowledge, we are exhibiting "implicit bias" (Banaji and Greenwald 2013). We all have these. These attitudes stem from our upbringing, exposure to media images, the history that we are taught (or not taught), literature we read, the music we listen to, the educational programs we attend, in other words, by the world around us.

For example, Black and Brown men are portrayed in the news and television series as dangerous and violent. At the same time, there has until recently been few depictions of Black and Brown men as intelligent, professional, and peaceful. Thus, when walking down a street at night, if we see a Black man, we may unconsciously grab our purse tighter or move to the other side of the sidewalk. These are unconscious reactions. Our unconscious identifies the Black body as dangerous and the White body as fragile. Stories of the damsel in distress always end with the knight rescuing her, and the knight always seems to be White, cisgender, and male. Unfortunately, these culturally entrenched beliefs affect the self-image that people of color have of themselves and can lead to "internalized oppression" (Pyke 2010).

Implicit bias can be life-threatening for those not belonging to the dominant group. In the United States, across almost every therapeutic intervention, ranging from the simplest diagnostic techniques and treatments to the most sophisticated ones, minoritized groups receive fewer procedures and poorer quality medical care than Whites even when factoring in insurance status, age, income, and illness severity (IOM 2003, 2002; American Medical Association 2009). Pain medication, for example, is prescribed far less for African Americans than for Whites (Hoffman et al. 2016). Few doctors intentionally overlook their Black patients—but the cultural norms permeate the whole medical system and influence individual decision making.

How Structures Sustain Bias and Racism

Legal and financial systems also play crucial roles in sustaining and reproducing unconscious and conscious biases. In the United States these biases have been supported by policies such as redlining aimed at keeping Blacks and other people of color "in their place."

Redlining gets its name from the practice of the Federal Housing Administration during the New Deal of drawing red lines on federal government maps that identify which neighborhoods were predominantly White and which were mostly Black and then refusing home loans to the latter areas while making them available to White neighborhoods (Rothstein 2017). Other groups such as Mexicans, Browns, and Asians were also excluded from loans by this mechanism.

Redlining was declared illegal by the United States Supreme Court in *Shelley v. Kraemer* (1968) but not before these policies, practices, and procedures had created serious and long-lasting impediments to equal access to housing, education, justice, and health. Redlining created a spinoff effect resulting in Black neighborhoods having—to this day—higher poverty rates, poorer funded schools, less healthcare access, and lower life expectancy than White neighborhoods (Yearby 2018; Strand 2017; Berkley and Letzing 2020; Williams and Collins 2013). This segregation also served as an obstacle to people from diverse groups coming together in meaningful ways, getting to know each other, and building community with individuals who did not share their same identity, religious beliefs, or race.

Individual biases and prejudices do not operate in a vacuum. Amy Cooper dialed 911 because she was confident that the legal system would be on her side. She knew just how the system operated to privilege her whiteness when in conflict with a Black man. When we work on individual conflicts, we need to be aware of the systems of oppression that may lie behind those conflicts and how these individual biases and systems operate to sustain racism.

Bias turns into racism when behaviors are institutionalized or embedded in our systems in ways that privilege an individual based on their race. This happens through both policies and unspoken norms. For example, the racist use of skin color to determine whether a policeman stops and frisks an individual likely results from implied norms and explicit policies. We may not consciously discriminate against others based on their race, but by benefiting from the policy (e.g. not getting stopped by police based on our race) or by our inaction in the face of it, we are still contributing to a racist system.

Race, Gender, and Colonialism

If we are to transform systems of oppression, we need to understand how these systems came about and how they function today. In the United States and Canada, colonialism, imperialism, and White male privilege are deeply rooted in their formation as nations. "We the people" in the US Constitution was not meant to include all the people; slaves, women, White men who owned no property, and BIPOC people were excluded. Despite its avowed commitment to freedom and democracy, at its core the US Constitution is a historically misogynist, elitist, and racist document. And yet it continues to be widely revered and seen as a model for other nations.

At the time of the ratification of the US Constitution in 1787, Article I, Section 2, established that for purposes of state representation in the House of Representatives each slave would count as three-fifths of a person, and in the mandatory census to take place every 10 years, Indigenous populations would be excluded. The three-fifths ratio had the effect of boosting slave-owning states' representation in Congress and Electoral College votes (Lepore 2019, 157) while institutionalizing the dehumanization of African Americans. Not until the passage of the 13th Amendment of the US Constitution, which repealed slavery, was this practice ended. Nowadays the three-fifths ratio has been replaced with gerrymandering, voting suppression, and a US Supreme Court that for the last half century has been eroding individual rights for the less privileged while protecting the wealthy and corporate America (Cohen 2020).

Women—also deemed as being "less than"—were not allowed to vote until 1920 with the ratification of the 19th Amendment of the US Constitution. The exclusion of participation in the political community was so brutal that Elizabeth Cady Stanton, a woman's rights activist of the 19th century, imagined the experience extending into her afterlife:

> "When I pass the gate of the celestials and good Peter asks me where I wish to sit, I will say, 'Anywhere so that I am neither a negro nor a woman. Confer on me, great angel, the glory of White Manhood, so that henceforth I may feel unlimited freedom."
> (Lepore, *These Truths: A History of the United States* [New York: WW Norton & Company, 2018], 314)

Likewise, the genocide of the Indigenous population, the invasion of Mexico in 1846, and the acquisitions of colonies in 1898 with the purchase of Puerto Rico, Guam, and the Philippines were all justified by supremacist ideology. The premise throughout was that BIPOC were property, savages undeserving of citizenship and democracy, and incapable of self-government. This is evidenced in legislative debates and US Supreme Court cases that to this day are cited and have not been revoked.

Imperialistic Ideology and Racism

Albert Memmi (1968, 194) argued that racist ideology is necessary to justify the conquest and oppression of others: "Underneath its masks, racism is the racist's way of giving himself absolution." Racism is a means of highlighting differences and using them to justify oppression. In the US colonies, White supremacy continues to be experienced daily. Although the 14th Amendment of the US Constitution, ratified in 1868, granted citizenship to all persons born in the United States—including former slaves—the US Supreme Court has repeatedly dodged ruling on whether this Amendment applies to those born in US-held colonies (Font-Guzmán 2015, 46). The inhabitants of the colonies were seen, and continue to be seen, as "less than."

Even well-intended North Americans (and residents of the colonies) may be falling into the trap of White supremacy when they advocate that the way to achieve equality for their colonial subjects is to grant US citizenship to their "fellow Americans." This framing was prevalent in Puerto Rico in the aftermath of Hurricane María. It promotes a narrative that sees the United States as a benevolent White savior coming to the rescue of the incompetent colonials who also happen to be people of color. Presenting citizenship as the solution to consequences of colonialism in fact "promotes Puerto Ricans' perpetual colonial status" and ignores the fact that Puerto Ricans—like many other US colonies and Indigenous nations—have never gone through a self-determination process (Font-Guzmán 2017). This blurs the distinction between a civil rights action and a self-determination process. In a civil rights action, there is a presumption that everyone is a citizen, and they should all have equal rights and responsibilities. But colonies do not have citizens; they have subjects who are expected to show allegiance to a nation without having full rights (Font-Guzmán 2015).

The process of self-determination is elusive. In the post-colonial era, we frequently obscure a colony's status as a possession of a controlling state by focusing on the wrong issue. Colonies need to first determine whether they wish to join the nation-state that is colonizing them or be their own sovereign nation-state. In other words, do they want the same rights to sit on the bus as all other passengers or do they want to drive their own bus? In the case of Puerto Rico, the political parties have organized according to their position on political status (status quo, independence, and statehood). This leaves Puerto Ricans asking the wrong questions. Instead of asking who they are, Puerto Ricans ask "who they are to the United States or in relation to the United States" (Font-Guzmán and Alemán 2010, 123).

The reason that the distinction between civil rights and self-determination is so difficult for many North Americans is that they choose not to see themselves as an empire. Most US citizens have no idea that the United States still owns colonies. Instead, they view the United States as a democratic republic which brings democracy to others. If you are a possession of the United States, you are likely to be viewed as being fortunate for your relationship with the motherland.

An estimated 4645 Puerto Ricans died in Hurricane María in 2018 (Kishore 2018). One of many excuses used by the United States for not delivering food, water, and medication to Puerto Ricans in a timely manner during the storm's aftermath was that

Puerto Rico is an island with many remote areas. How could a nation accustomed to setting up military field hospitals in remote war zones honestly claim that they could not come to assist people living in an island that is 100 by 35 miles?

Instead, Puerto Ricans organized to support each other. They installed electrical posts and provided each other with food and water as well as many other services that the government should have provided. In the process many Puerto Ricans—me (Jackie) included—ended up despising the word "resilience" to describe the actions that Puerto Ricans took to restore some sort of stability after the storm. The initial infatuation with resilience was captured in the slogan "Puerto Rico se levanta" (Puerto Rico will rise). Many Puerto Ricans began to challenge this rhetoric, which served as a way of insinuating that anyone who could not manage the situation was somehow weak. It also failed to hold the state and federal government accountable for the structural violence that occurred before and after the storm (Bonilla and Lebrón 2019, 3).

The use of words such as "resilience," "courage," and "bravery" is often a distraction from the need for systemic change. The efforts of minoritized groups in the face of such crises (Hurricane Katrina provides another example) are not simply acts of "resilience." They are also a de facto uprising against an oppressive system. Pablo Marcano, world-renowned Puerto Rican painter, describes his experience of structural violence that accompanies living in a colony:

> "I have a painting of a woman washing her hair and her hair was full of thorns; it was like a crown of thorns. And I believe that this visual metaphor depicts the colonial condition on one end, but also the willingness of the Puerto Rican people to struggle and resist. Because every day we wake up and it is as if we have to assert who we are day after day; we see ourselves in a mirror, we see that we are there, that we exist in spite

of the crown of thorns that we have over our head, that we exist. And we are willing to continue to wash our hair, in spite of the fact that we have not been able to remove the crown of thorns."

(Font-Guzmán, *Experiencing Puerto Rican Citizenship and Cultural Nationalism* [New York: Palgrave Macmillan, 2015], 52–53)

Immerwhar (2019, 19) in his book *How to Hide an Empire* discusses how the logo map of the United States hides all its overseas possessions, giving its citizens a "truncated view" of their own history. This view of US history prevents the nation and its people from seeing how slavery and racism are consequences of being an empire. It also erases the violence the United States has inflicted upon its colonies and suppresses the history of the colonies' struggles against their colonial status.

To eradicate racism, colonial powers must come to terms with the fact that they are empires. Racism and slavery emanate from the imperialistic and colonizing mindset of being superior to "others" who are not White. Erasing the essential role of colonialism in our history only perpetuates White supremacy.

A Note About Performativity, Virtue Signaling, and Change

Discussing intersectionality, race, gender, and all the "isms" that are implicit is fraught. One troubling dynamic is that our capacity to learn the "right language," to make sure we show how clued we are, may outpace our genuine efforts to bring about change. Posting our concerns on social media is not the same as participating in a movement. Alicia Garza, a founder of the Black Lives Matter movement, talks about what it means to build a movement for change:

". . . movements are not just visible or viral—they com-
prise people who are dedicated to achieving some kind
of change. The change they (and we) seek cannot be
accomplished by something going viral. The change
we seek can only be accomplished through sustained
organizing."

(Garza, *The Purpose of Power: How We Come
Together When We Fall Down* [New York: One World,
2020], 141)

This does not mean posting anti-racist thoughts on social media
is a bad thing. It is important to declare our commitment to looking at our own biases, being good allies, and calling out behavior
that contributes to oppression. The language we use is important
and sometimes the path to change begins with public statements
that are supportive of change. But if it stops there, if we perform,
signal, and post but don't continue to work to expand our awareness and to disrupt systems of oppression, then performativity can
become a way of taking pressure off a system rather than working
to change it.

In that spirit, we turn our attention to what constructive
engagement with conflict really means.

chapter four

constructive engagement

"The only sensible and intelligent way of resolving differences and clashes of interests, whether between individuals or nations, is through dialogue."

—The Dalai Lama

"When angry, count to four; when very angry, swear."

—Mark Twain

Constructive conflict engagement is the common goal that conflict interveners, advocates for social change, and peace builders share. At our best, none of us in any of these roles wants to suppress essential conflict or take away anyone's legitimate voice. Conflict specialists may concentrate on how to create the space for people to work on the specific issues that divide them. Change advocates may emphasize the need for system change and how to build the personal connections and structures that can accomplish this. Peace builders may focus on "positive peace," how to address the most basic needs people and societies have that if met will lay the groundwork for not only the end of hostilities but a long-term framework for harmony. Mediators may look for opportunities to carve out negotiated solutions to divisive issues.

None of these goals can be met without confronting the essential role of conflict. Without an effective approach to confronting our differences over time in a way that is powerful and yet constructive, the issues that divide us will continue to do so, significant social change will not be achieved, and peace will prove elusive or ephemeral. But what do we mean by constructive engagement and how do we achieve it? And where does the ubiquitous call for dialogue fit into this picture? We start with exploring just what we mean by constructive conflict engagement (and how we can separate it from the regressive way the call for constructive engagement sometimes plays out).

What Is Constructive Conflict Engagement?

Bernie: Some of the hardest moments I have faced as a third party involve having to handle angry personal attacks that people level at each other. The challenge has been deterring interactions from becoming so personal and insulting that any constructive conversation becomes impossible, while realizing that if these conversations are redirected or cut off, the emotional and often substantive heart of a dispute will remain buried. I can try to reframe all I want, but this dilemma will not simply disappear. For example, consider this reconstructed interchange from a policy dialogue on hunting and trapping.

Trapping enthusiast: Let me explain how we use traps and how we minimize pain and suffering for the animals we are trapping.

Animal rights activist: Well let me explain something—you are a murderer, your group are murderers, and what you are describing is murder! How can you live with yourselves?

Trapping enthusiast: And you are a self-righteous elitist who has never had to live off the land to feed your family.

The facilitator (me): Clearly you have profoundly different values about this and I suspect you will continue to hold these. We should talk about these values and how each of you came to them, but calling each other names isn't going to help. What we can do is listen to each other's stories and see whether there are some beliefs we share and areas of policy that might be worthwhile trying to come to agreement about.

I succeeded in keeping the discussion going, and some fairly general agreements about policies and principles were reached. But meaningful communication about genuine differences did not occur. For these stakeholders, giving voice to their anger was an essential part of bearing witness to their beliefs and worldview. But it also made genuine conversation very difficult. And neither side was convinced of the value of engaging in this process to begin with.

In retrospect, I wish I had asked them to speak more about how angry they were and to share more of their stories. That may have blown up the whole process, but by redirecting it, I interfered with an opportunity to get closer to the heart of the issue. Instead, the group ended up working on the periphery of their most meaningful differences and made very little inroad into the essential conflict. I ended up feeling, agreements or not, that this process failed to reach its potential. Was this constructive engagement or conflict avoidance? Or both?

Trying to encourage a constructive approach to conflict based on profound differences of values and worldviews is a complex and often daunting challenge. But it is not impossible. Some of the most powerful experiences of interpersonal and intergroup inter-action occur when we take the plunge into our most troubling differences and find ourselves in an honest if at times painful inter-change. For example:

Bernie:

- Talking to supporters of the war in Vietnam while I was devoting all my energies to opposing it.

- Participating (really fomenting) a discussion between Roma and Slavic ethnic groups about racist beliefs and practices toward the Roma.

- Confronting sexist statements and misogynist jokes among a group of male friends.

Jackie:

- Taking on a family member (whom I care deeply about) who argued that same-sex relationships are sinful, a belief I am in profound disagreement with.

- Engaging with a dear friend who favors the full annexation of Puerto Rico into the United States, something I have spent my life opposing.

- Advocating for the right of prisoners to have the best healthcare service available in a meeting with government representatives who argued that prisoners should not have better healthcare than the population at large.

We are drawn to building narratives with neat endings. A social wrong has been righted. A serious conflict has been resolved. A fractured relationship has been repaired. But the process of dealing with conflict is mostly messier than that, and often the most constructive goal is to engage rather than resolve, to dive into our differences without expecting to emerge with everything worked out.

Constructive engagement means connecting with those we are in conflict with—to argue, fight, listen, explain, question, and respond. We hope that in the process we obtain a deeper understanding of the issues, of each other, and of ourselves, and ultimately that understanding leads to action. As we engage, we may chip away at our differences and reach some agreements, but if we focus exclusively on that, we are likely to forgo the opportunity to address the most important and troubling elements of the conflict. When conflict engagement is truly constructive, it moves us forward to better understanding, less destructive behaviors, and improved communication. Sometimes, this can lead to the development of genuine friendships even as important elements of a conflict continue. At other times, our efforts at engagement may drive us further apart.

Constructive engagement does not imply minimizing conflict nor does it preclude reaching agreements. The fundamental goal of engagement efforts is to look at a conflict squarely, to combat our tendencies to avoid conflict, and to devote our attention to trying to understand the nature of our differences. But it does not mean giving up our values or essential goals in the name of understanding each other. Constructive engagement has at times been used as a rubric for avoiding taking significant action to confront injustice. For example, Ronald Reagan's refusal to participate in the boycott of South Africa in the name of "constructive engagement" was deemed to have undercut the anti-apartheid movement and enabled the continuation of racist policies (Elliott 2011). In that case, as in others, the term was used for a policy that did not address the fundamental issues at stake nor the vast power differentials involved.

The Limits of Understanding

> "By refraining from fully understanding and staying with uncertainty, I could connect with those who were different without relating them to my norm and thus violently reducing them to objects in need of being understood."
>
> (Font-Guzmán, "Personal Reflection on 50 Years of Loving: Creating Spaces of Differences by Demanding 'The Right to Opacity'" [*Creighton Law Review*, 50 no. 3, 2017b], 638)

Engagement is not just about understanding and sometimes understanding is not only an elusive but also an inappropriate goal. We need to have the humility to accept that we will never fully understand the impact that our differences have in our daily lives. As hard as we try, it is impossible to "stand in someone else's shoes." They will not fit and even if they do, the experience will be different. This requires us to have the courage to recognize and name the difference before we understand how those differences play out. Constructive engagement often requires staying with uncertainty.

Our obsession with trying to "understand" each other can become an obstacle to celebrating our differences. Édouard Glissant (2010, 189)—prominent poet and philosopher from Martinique—talks about the "right to opacity," the right to not be understood. As a woman from the Caribbean I (Jackie) have frequently been frustrated when the need of those with colonial power over us to understand becomes an excuse for inaction and a deterrent to advancing respect and social justice.

Our goal ought to be finding a way to move forward together despite the inevitable limits on our understanding.

Constructive Engagement and Systems Change

A premature focus on constructive engagement in the absence of clear efforts to promote systems change and to develop the tools, analysis, and social movements necessary to do so can perpetuate an oppressive system. For engagement to be truly constructive, oppressive power dynamics must be challenged. We are concerned with a reflexive call for engagement and dialogue in the absence of serious efforts to disrupt systems that maintain the status quo. But we also believe that constructive engagement is a necessary element of the change process at the right time, with the right people, and in the right way.

Constructive engagement efforts are themselves complex systems. In a study on constructive engagement in protracted social conflict, Coleman et al. (2012) viewed constructive engagement as a dynamical process (as is protracted conflict) and defined it as: "the problem of getting the necessary disputants and stakeholders actively involved in a constructive, nonviolent process and ultimately maintaining their commitment to such a process" (pp. 27–28). Their view of engagement emphasizes its capacity to alter the dynamics of an entrenched conflict by changing the characteristics of the system of interactions that define that conflict. We discuss these concepts further in Chapter 6.

Constructive escalation is often essential to conflict engagement, and in that sense strategic disruption is an important element as well. System disruption is an uncertain process, but so is conflict engagement more generally. "Do no harm" as a mantra does not work here. If we are to try to take on our differences, we will sometimes make things worse. If we are unwilling to risk this, we commit ourselves to shallow interactions and the continuation of the status quo. We have agency, however. We can make a difference, no matter what role we are in, in guiding conflict interactions in constructive directions.

What Makes Engagement Constructive?

With the understanding of the tension but also the synergy between constructive engagement and strategic disruption, we propose some essential elements to consider in assessing engagement efforts. Ideally, constructive engagement is:

- *Grounded in our values about outcome, structure, and process*: These values must be reflected in our entire approach—in the goals we are pursuing, the way we are conducting ourselves, and the structures we are creating. If these structures are not democratic, transparent, and non-hierarchical, they will undercut the very causes we seek to promote.

- *Open to engaging with alternative worldviews*: Worldview is the cognitive framework through which we interpret and make sense of reality (Nash 1992, 16). We do not have to accept other ideologies, but we need to be able to identify conflicts that arise out of a clash of worldviews and search

for a way to discuss our differences on this basic level
(Docherty 2001, 53).

- *Committed to relationship building*: A sustained effort at
  conflict engagement (and strategic disruption) requires that
  we nurture quality relationships with others and expand
  our network of allies. But it also is essential to build relationships across our differences. This does not mean we
  have to become friends with racists, for example, but if we
  are trying to understand their motivations and life experiences and share our stories with them, we have to create a
  relational space to do so.

- *Sustainable*: Serious engagement takes time. Not every effort
  starts out with a long-term commitment to continue an
  interaction, but maintaining an openness to that potential
  and an awareness of what that might demand is important.

- *Attentive to power dynamics*: All conflicts involve an exer-
  tion of some form of power and have implications for how
  power dynamics can change as a result of how the conflict
  plays out (see the section entitled "Three Essential Features
  of Meaningful Dialogue"). Of course, choosing not to participate in a dialogue will also alter power relationships.

- *Emotionally authentic*: An important source of our power
  is emotional. Our determination, optimism, caring, anger,
  and love are part of who we are and of how we relate to the
  world. And yet disempowered groups, especially women
  and people of color, are often put in the position of having
  to suppress or hide their emotions. Creating a space where
  all people can speak and act with emotional authenticity
  even when those feelings are not "nice" is essential to the
  authenticity and effectiveness of conflict engagement.

- *Flexible*: Forethought helps; rigidity does not. Constructive engagement is dynamic. The effectiveness of an effort depends on the interaction of the participants, the influence of those outside of the process, external circumstances, and much more.

- *Realistic but also hopeful*: Neither naïve optimism nor cynical pessimism are compatible with constructive engagement (see the section entitled "Optimism and Realism About Social Change"). A clear-eyed view of the difficulties together with a belief in our capacity to make a difference make engagement efforts viable and sustainable.

- *Grounded in effective communication practices*: Engagement and dialogue are about communication—whether direct or indirect, synchronous or asynchronous, in person or virtual, facilitated or self-directed. The approaches to constructive engagement are myriad but all require good communications skills and processes.

- *Deliberate about process*: Effective engagement does not require elaborate processes, but process matters. This means paying attention to whether a process is working for all participants, moving a conversation forward, and allowing space for diverse perspectives as well as the depth of feelings involved.

- *Attuned to diversity*: It should be obvious that interaction about diversity requires attention to different norms and practices about how to interact across our diversity of backgrounds and power differentials. What we may think of as a universally normative value about how to interact might in fact be very culturally specific. Diversity without a sense of belongingness will not allow for active participation from everyone.

- *Committed to nonviolent approaches:* Constructive conflict interactions almost by definition must be nonviolent, but the expressed commitment to nonviolence is itself an important contributor to a meaningful interaction across our differences.

Lest the list seem too daunting, we need to realize that no engagement effort is perfect, no matter how carefully we plan or how clear we are about our purpose. These are hallmarks of constructive engagement processes—criteria to weigh in considering, planning, conducting, and assessing them. We discuss more specific criteria for dialogue next.

The Uses and Misuses of Dialogue

Constructive conflict engagement comes in many guises, but it mostly comes down to some form of dialogue. Dialogue processes— the intentional, planned, and focused interchanges among people with diverse points of view—have the potential to advance social justice efforts, hinder them, or sometimes do a bit of both.

As we have discussed previously, the default position so many of us take when faced with our most troubling conflicts is to suggest that we talk. Dialogue if timed well, designed with wisdom, and conducted with skill can be very powerful, and it is an important element of our most important civic processes. But those are big ifs. Dialogue in all its many guises can be a means of engaging in conflict or avoiding it.

Dialogue implies an intentionality, a two-wayedness, and a willingness to tackle difficult issues. One organization that promotes dialogue distinguishes between dialogue and conversation:

"When we refer to the term 'dialogue' we are usually suggesting a richer and deeper outcome to a conversation; one that is open and sincere. We expect more from dialogue than we do from an ordinary conversation, discussion or debate. In dialogue, we expect the means to be collaborative and the outcome to be a new sense of mutual understanding as a result of the exchange of giving and taking."

(Bramble, "What Is at the Heart of Creative
Dialogue" [*Leading Creatively*, June 2017])

Let's look at a specific example of a carefully constructed dialogue to consider how dialogues can contribute to building movements for change.

Talking About Access to Justice

The justice system across the common law world (and elsewhere) faces an enormous but until recently largely ignored challenge in providing meaningful access to justice. This challenge stems from the escalating cost of legal representation. Simply put, lawyers are too expensive for most people to afford. Professor Gillian Hadfield has argued:

"... we have allowed tremendously complex legal processes to develop that exploit the fact that the vast majority of people cannot manage tremendously complex legal processes."

(Hadfield, Twitter post, January 29, 2018)

As a result, 50% of family court and 30% of the civil court cases in the United States and Canada involve *self-represented litigants* (SRLs). In urban courts these numbers are often considerably higher (80% in some family courts). This phenomenon has not only overwhelmed the court system but has led to horrific results for many who are forced to represent themselves (Macfarlane 2013). To understand this phenomenon, Professor Julie Macfarlane conducted the National Self-Represented Litigants Study from 2011 to 2013, the first significant effort to understand the experience from the point of view of SRLs themselves. The SRL Study raised significant questions about how to address this deeply institution-alized source of injustice.

Macfarlane and her staff decided to organize a "dialogue event" to bring together 45 lawyers, judges, court staff, and other repre-sentatives of the legal system with 15 self-represented litigants from across Canada. This three-day event (May 9–11, 2013) trans-formed the views of participants from the justice system about what impelled SRLs to represent themselves and what they experienced in doing so. Previously, many attendees felt that SRLs were moti-vated by a distrust of lawyers and an angry belief that they could do a better job representing themselves. But the study and the presentations by SRLs made it clear that cost was the fundamental problem causing self-representation.

In addition to changing attitudes and perceptions, the event led to the creation of the National Self-Represented Litigants Project, which since 2013 has produced additional reports, resources for SRLs, advocacy for SRL-friendly policies and prac-tices in the courts, and perhaps most importantly has begun to provide SRLs with a genuine voice in the discussion of access to justice.

The SRL Dialogue is an example of how dialogue and strategic disruption can come together. The response of the legal system gives testimony to the disruptive nature of this process. System players (e.g. law societies and judicial institutes) alternated between ignor-ing the results of the study, attacking them, and arguing that the message has been heard and the system is taking care of the prob-lem. But while the problem will not easily disappear, the first step to systems change has now occurred—the issue has been named and acknowledged, and it is being widely discussed.

What makes this event so interesting was how it combined the best elements of dialogue with intentional efforts at disruption. For example:

- SRLs were funded to attend from across Canada. They had never been part of such discussions.

- Participants wore nametags containing only their first name so to begin with no one could be sure if they were talking to a judge, a legal services administrator, a professor, a lawyer, or an SRL.

- Small-group sessions, meals, seating arrangements, and panels were organized to involve legal professionals and SRLs in both facilitated and informal discussions.

- Facilitators (Bernie was one) were careful to make sure that no one group or individual dominated the discussion.

- The intention was dialogue, not agreement, and the plan to form an ongoing project emerged from the discussions. However, there were decision makers in the room (e.g. the dean of the law school where the project is located and the event took place, the director of the project, and leaders of potential funding organizations) who were in a position to make this happen.

The stated purpose of this event was to increase understanding and to generate ideas for how to respond to the needs of SRLs, but the overall intent of the effort was system change.

Three Essential Features of Meaningful Dialogue

What makes for effective dialogue? Three essential characteristics seem both characteristic and essential to meaningful interchanges across significant differences. Let's look at all three.

Naming the Elephant "You cannot fight for a freedom you have failed to identify."

(Zadie Smith, *Feel Free: Essays*
[New York: Penguin Press, 2018], xviii)

We have both participated in time-consuming and elaborately planned dialogue processes that avoided naming the most serious and painful element of a conflict and therefore were at best unsatisfying. Often this was about race or gender. Yet when the process allows or even insists that the hardest issues be identified, amazing things can happen.

Naming can be both simple and extremely difficult. Both parties in the hunting and trapping dialogue were in their own way trying to name the issue that was most important to them. The animal rights activists thought they were trying to prevent slaughter. The trappers thought they were defending their way of life. How could they name these issues in an authentic way? How could they have been best helped to do so? There may have been almost no space to name these in a way that they all would accept other than by reducing them to such vague generalities as to make them almost meaningless. But if that were the case, then it is unlikely that this dialogue would be worth the effort.

Imagine, instead, that we could have helped the groups to be out front that they viewed each other as immoral and asked them to consider whether they still wanted to understand where the other was coming from. That may have resulted in a narrowing of the conflict, a richer description of the issues in contention, or a breakdown in the stereotypes they were holding about each other. While this might only have led to more understanding of exactly why it was so difficult to find any common ground, perhaps that, too, would be of value. And of course, it could have led to more ad homonym attacks and further deterioration of their ability to communicate.

Four principles help to understand what is essential to naming:

- Naming is about saying what is most important to each of the participants.

- Values are part of naming. The more people give voice to what they believe in, as opposed to focusing on what they are against, the easier it will be to find the common space necessary for dialogue. (I may be against racism, but I am also for equality. I may be against killing animals but also for respect for all living things.) But positive framing alone will not work if the essential value and meaning is tied to what we do not like or want.

- Underneath most of our values (and interests) are other values. Pushing for the deeper values is what makes dialogue rich. (Why are we for equal employment opportunities? Because we believe everyone should be given a fair chance. Why is that important?) As we push for our deeper values, we often discover surprising areas of agreement that we may not have perceived, and we may open the door to storytelling.

- It's not for any of us to name the issue that is important to others. We can help each other articulate our issues as each of us sees them, but we should remember what is important here—naming is about how each participant views the issues, not about what we think they think or ought to think.

Telling Our Stories "[Effective stories] changed you . . . , made the world seem to be telling a different, more interesting story, a story in which you might play a meaningful part, and in which you had responsibilities."
(Saunders, *A Swim in a Pond in The Rain; In Which Four Russians Give a Master Class on Writing, Reading, and Life* [New York: Random House, 2021], 5)

Storytelling can be a path to depth and understanding of diverse truths and experiences. Our most meaningful exchanges with each other occur in the form of sharing stories—and connecting to the stories others are sharing with us. We tell many different kinds of stories, for example, ones that disclose our journey, the myths that motivate us, the people we admire (or detest), and stories that uplift, amuse, or build on others' stories. But the essence of all powerful stories is that they reveal something important about who we are and in so doing allow us to connect more fully with each other.

Effective dialogue requires a safe space and structure for story-telling. When people share a counter-story (one that threatens a dominant narrative), they often pay a very high price. People who share stories of sexual harassment or racism are often subjected to marginalization, trauma, demotion, and dismissal even when using channels supposedly set up for this very purpose. Counter-stories have a high potential to challenge the status quo and connect us with those who are different. And yet, they are usually suppressed, ignored, or discouraged by those in positions of power. The challenge that conflict engagement practitioners and activists face in this regard is how to set up powerful processes for sharing potentially volatile stories that are attentive to the safety of those sharing the story, encourage those with power to listen (without being defensive if possible), and open the door for further dialogue.

Talking circles, used by many Indigenous groups in North America to discuss important and potentially divisive issues, offer a powerful approach to doing just that. Talking circles vary considerably but are generally characterized by participants sitting in a circle and passing a talking stick from one participant to the next. When holding the talking stick, the participant can speak as long as they feel they need to share their perspective and tell their story. The stick continues to be passed around the circle until everyone feels they have expressed what is important to them. This approach has been adapted by many restorative justice programs.

Unfortunately, in most of our business or civic interactions, not only is there no space for meaningful storytelling, but it is also counter-normative. When we have worked on cross-cultural conflict, for example, between businesses and Indigenous communities, finding ways to allow for genuine sharing of stories has often been challenging. Business groups want to tell a story about what makes business work and view the more deliberate and personal storytelling approach of First Nations people as a distraction from what is important. The task of those facilitating such exchanges is to recognize the needs of both groups while encouraging significant and meaningful storytelling to occur.

The potential of storytelling, and of dialogue more generally, is not just to increase our understanding of each other, but to participate in a reciprocal process of change. Stories help us see our differences through new frames and build relationships across intersecting values They open the possibility for a "moving forward together" story to emerge. For example, coming-out stories were at the core of how LGBTQIA+ were able to advance legal rights like the right to marriage, connect with those who perceived them as the "other," and advance policy changes in record time (Strand 2011; Vedantam 2019). Stories of the AIDS epidemic also prompted gay people to publicly grapple with the vulnerability of surviving at the margins of society and of not having legal rights such as making medical decisions on behalf of their partners. This led to a powerful narrative shift in most of the gay community from "leave us alone" toward "we want full membership in society" (Vedantam 2019).

Attending to Power Dynamics. The surest way to counteract the potential for dialogue to reinforce an oppressive status quo is to confront the power dynamics embedded in all dialogues (really in all human interactions). The challenge here is not to balance power, or even to create a totally level playing field. That is not possible—or even meaningful. No playing field is totally level. Power is never truly balanced. The question instead is whether the effort at dialogue or collaboration contributes to an oppressive power differential.

Conflict engagement efforts seldom occur under ideal circumstances, and the decision to engage in dialogue often cuts in conflicting directions. We may find ourselves engaging in a dialogue that has the potential to simultaneously build a social movement and undercut it. Or we may be involved in political actions that impede the workings of a potentially valuable dialogue.

For this reason, different organizations committed to the same overall goals often emphasize different elements of engagement. In the struggle for racial justice, the NAACP has historically emphasized legal action and negotiation. SNCC and CORE were more focused on disruption through protests. Similar differences can be seen among different environmental organizations (e.g. the Environmental Defense Fund and Greenpeace).

This division of roles may make strategic sense, but creates two problems. One is that the tension between these approaches to change inevitably creates strain among the organizations committed to them—and these can be dysfunctional for the overall effort. Also, whether one is oriented to disruption or negotiation, the need to integrate a range of conflict engagement strategies remains. Activists are always making choices as to whether to engage in dialogue, to search for what are at best short-term or partial solutions, or to escalate a conflict. These approaches can be both totally intertwined and very different. This was the situation that Gandhi faced in his struggle for Indian independence discussed in Chapter 1.

Sometimes, groups with an overt commitment to disruption can frame their demands or portray their opponents in ways that preclude or at least complicate the future potential to engage or negotiate. On the other hand, those who see the answer to all conflict as constructive engagement or negotiated resolution often dismiss or undercut activists' efforts to build a powerful movement for change. For example, consider a well-intentioned effort to promote a dialogue about confederate symbols and statues. At the right time, this might be a useful undertaking. But asking movement leaders who have been oppressed by a White power structure to try to work in a collaborative way with those who cling to monuments to the Confederacy is fraught at best. Such a request can easily undercut the efforts to mobilize and energize a movement for change.

Assessing the Potential of Dialogue

How can we tell if a dialogue process will contribute to a social change effort in a meaningful way? We can never know for sure, and entering into one is often a leap of faith that good things can happen. Frequently they do, but the downsides we have discussed may be present as well. Certain questions can help gauge the potential of a process:

- *Who is convening and facilitating the dialogue?* The issues here are transparency, credibility, and purpose. Trained facilitators and process designers can be beneficial, but their purpose and the participants' purpose need to be complementary. If we convene or facilitate a process where our purpose is to move a policy forward (as in the trapping example at the beginning of this chapter) while participants are more interested in bearing witness to their most fervent beliefs, we either need to revise our goals or question the legitimacy of the effort.

- *How is the purpose defined?* Sometimes, the most effective and subtle way for a dominant group to exercise its power is through controlling how a problem is defined. Are we trying to mitigate the efforts of a controversial mine or question whether it should exist? Are we trying to treat everyone the same in how we administer justice, decide on university admissions, or hire staff or do we seek to counteract the structural sources of discrimination that lead to unjust outcomes? Purpose is often defined by the questions being raised, which can seem balanced, even though embedded within them are presumptions of purpose and narrative.

- *Who is coming (and who decides who is coming)?* Are key stakeholder groups not only invited to attend, but involved in a meaningful and effective way? Are they involved in process design and evaluation? In deciding who comes? Who facilitates? Who evaluates? Are key decision makers present? Are there participants who are in a position to fund or implement recommendations that may come out of a dialogue?

- *How appropriately is the effort resourced?* Dialogues don't necessarily need to be richly funded—and requiring that can introduce a major power discrepancy. But if some groups have access to experts, data, and technology and others do not, the resultant power differentials are likely to be problematic. Time is also a resource. Does the process take into account the different capacity of people to participate? Community members may have to arrange for days off or for child care to attend, while corporate or governmental participants are paid for their time and compensated for their expenses.

- *Is the process structured to give everyone a meaningful voice? Are issues of gender, culture, or race taken into account?* This is not just about how much time is allocated for this purpose, but whether the process allows for different styles of participating, different languages, and different comfort levels with speaking in large groups.

- *What outcomes are participants expecting and how realistic are these?* Is there pressure to reach agreements—from organizers or participants? Or the reverse—an expectation that the dialogue will be about exchange but not outcomes? Are there contradictory expectations?

- *What will happen next?* Will the discussion, the areas of agreement or disagreement, the issues and concerns raised, and the successes and shortcomings of the effort be memorialized in a meaningful, appropriate, and accessible way?

Finding Solutions

We have been focusing on constructive engagement, dialogue, and strategic disruption. But what about actually trying to solve some problems along the way? What is wrong with coming up with agreements on issues that have been contentious? The short answer is nothing unless doing so is a means of avoiding the real conflict and undercutting the capacity of social movements to promote justice.

In fact, making progress through achieving solutions to specific elements of a conflict—either agreed upon or wrested from the powers that be through collective action—is essential to energizing and sustaining social movements. Sometimes these outcomes are performative or transitory (e.g. the many instances of commissions to investigate gun violence, policing practices, or sexual abuse), but at other times they represent important steps forward (the Voting Rights Act of 1965).

In our work as mediators, we have often observed that a laser-like focus on potential areas of agreement can lead to the abandonment of efforts to deal with the deeper issues that may be the most important. This focus can suppress the emotional dimension of a conflict, lead to frayed relationships, and reinforce ongoing patterns of oppression. And when conducted with an expectation of confidentiality and connected to nondisclosure agreements, resolution efforts can readily isolate victims of abuse and force a focus on specific instances of misbehavior rather than systemic patterns.

For example:

- Handling each complaint of sexual abuse separately and failing to deal with the systemic problems in religious institutions, businesses, schools, sports, or entertainment.

- Settling medical malpractice claims confidentially and individually rather than considering the practices and power structures that lead to poor overall patient care.

- Focusing on specific sources of water pollution rather than on industry-wide practices that endanger entire watersheds.

- Using legalistic processes such as Title IX to address issues related to hostile environments in academic institutions but avoiding the systemic issues and a culture of abuse that is not adequately addressed through such processes.

We are not against seizing the moment to obtain progress on important issues, and as we further discuss in the next chapter, this can be critical to growing a movement. There is no necessary contradiction between focusing on agreements while connecting to systemic problems—if we remain conscious of the need to do so. But without that, genuine engagement can be forestalled by "settlement fever"—a rush to solutions that precludes genuine dialogue. This critique of settlement processes is not a new one. Many conflict intervention specialists have pointed out the need to get beyond an immediate and transactional focus if these processes are to attain their potential for achieving meaningful resolution and dealing with the relational aspects of conflict (see Bush and Folger 2005; Cloke 2001; Della Noce 1999; Rothman 1997). Common to these critiques is a focus on the interpersonal or community building potential that collaborative processes can have if their focus extends beyond the immediate resolution of specific issues.

Optimism and Realism About System Change

"I'm a pessimist because of intelligence, but an optimist
because of will."
(Antonio Gramsci, "Letters from Prison," 1929,
quoted in Frank Rosengarten, *The Revolutionary
Marxism of Antonio Gramsci* [Brill, 2013])

As we discuss what makes for constructive engagement and the appropriate use of dialogue, we face the daunting complexity of achieving system change. Our doubts about whether anything we do will make a difference can be enormous impediments to change. Oppressive systems commonly promote the belief that fundamental change is impossible. Buying into this can easily become a self-fulfilling prophecy and remaining optimistic is a challenge we all face. If we think the environment is doomed and therefore do nothing, it is in fact doomed. But naiveté is also an obstacle. System change requires a long-term commitment, and along with moments of amazing progress, change efforts will encounter serious and sometimes long-lasting setbacks. We need to remain clear-eyed about what we are up against.

We write this book in the belief that fundamental system change is not only possible but inevitable. We also know that systems can change for the worse, that racism and misogyny have been with us for seemingly ever, that climate change seems impossible to avoid, and that the systems that perpetuate these problems are powerful and entrenched. But systems do change. The arc of history does bend toward justice, and social movements have an immense potential to make a difference.

We are not naïve about the obstacles to change but neither do we believe that we are doomed. We believe optimism about the potential for building a less racist, more peaceful, and more sustainable world is warranted. We also believe it is a moral necessity.

100 THE NEUTRALITY TRAP

As Bernie has previously argued (Mayer 2015), authentic optimism requires realism, and realism to be realistic requires optimism. Pessimism may be safer. It may inoculate us against disappointment and protect us against accusations of being dangerously naïve. But as an approach to the world we live in, a descent into pessimism is no more genuinely realistic than unmoderated optimism. The morass of ethnic conflict in the Middle East, for example, is deeply entrenched and at times seemingly insurmountable, particularly as we see the region descend into ever-worsening cycles of violence and repression. But circumstances are evolving, systemic pressures for improvement are not going away, and as hopeless as things may seem now, change is inevitable. Our world is getting warmer, and we are already facing very serious consequences, perhaps including the COVID-19 epidemic. But we can still take action to mitigate some of its worst effects. While rejecting "empty optimism," Greta Thunberg says, "If we humans would actually start treating the climate crisis like a crisis, we could really change things" (quoted in Widdicome 2021).

To face the daunting obstacles to social change in a way that is both optimistic and realistic, we have to delve into the nature of long-term conflicts, the challenges they pose, and the ways in which these can be met. We turn to these challenges in the next chapter.

part two

deepening conflict

chapter five

the hope and challenge of enduring conflict

"Without looking forward to an extremity of this kind [despotism] (which nevertheless ought not to be entirely out of sight), the common and continual mischiefs of the spirit of party are sufficient to make it the interest and duty of a wise people to discourage and restrain it. It serves always to distract the public councils and enfeeble the public administration. It agitates the community with ill-founded jealousies and false alarms, kindles the animosity of one part against another, foments occasionally riot and insurrection. It opens the door to foreign influence and corruption, which finds a facilitated access to the government itself through the channels of party passions."

—George Washington, "Farewell Address"

"…partisanship rips at the bonds of affection that tie the country state to state, political party to political party, citizen to citizen."

—Joe Biden

With only the slightest modernization of syntax, Washington's famous admonition about the danger of factions could be about the perils of our time. "False alarms," "enfeebled public administration," "riot and insurrection," "foreign influence and corruption," these warnings from 225 years ago seem written for today. And Joe Biden appears to agree.

Our most important conflicts do not readily disappear. How they manifest themselves changes over time as do the players, location, and impact, but their roots are deep, and they stay with us as long as their structural foundations remain. This does not mean that there is no progress along the way, and it certainly does not mean that we are helpless to make a difference. But if we are looking to make progress on foundational problems such as racism, sexism, sustainability, or the tensions between our commitment to our community and our desire for personal freedom, we have to be prepared for an extended effort with uncertain and incremental results.

For example, if we consider the conflict generated by the impact of policing practices on people of color, we have to face the deeply entrenched nature of this issue. We may believe that with enough publicity, with the very public conviction of police officers (e.g. Derek Chauvin) responsible for the killing of Black or Hispanic youth, and with increased oversight processes, we can finally solve this painful manifestation of racism. But as important as those steps are, policing practices and racial profiling are rooted deeply in our culture and history. An enduring conflict elicits a long-term struggle for change. To achieve the structural change necessary to address the sources of this conflict, our very understanding of what makes communities safe for everyone needs to broaden. We need to expand mental health and substance abuse services, reform hiring and accountability procedures, address educational and housing inequities, confront our addiction to guns, and address widely held stereotypes about race and class.

Therein lies both the hope and challenge presented by enduring conflicts. Hopeful because they provide an entry into dealing with our most significant social problems; challenging because the progress is hard to come by, episodic (often slow, sometimes dramatic), and always partial.

So many of our greatest problems are the long-term effects of colonialism, slavery, patriarchy, and an economic system that requires continuous increases in productivity to work. These are deep roots indeed, and it can be exhausting and dispiriting to confront them. Especially since there is no obvious way to work on the grand scale that this framing implies. As suggested in Chapter 1, action needs to be targeted, localized, and tactical. But our understanding of the problem needs to match its scale, or our strategic approach will be flawed. One way to get at this is to consider the tensions and interconnectedness between short-term disputes and deeply entrenched divisions, between small issues and enormous social problems, between conflicts that are amenable to resolution and those that even with the best of intentions and processes may evolve but won't end. Conflict interveners confront these tensions constantly. So do activists.

The Faces of Conflict

For a very short period in our history, after the Supreme Court's ruling in *Roe v. Wade*, the issue of reproductive rights seemed headed if not for resolution at least for a stable equilibrium. Within certain limits, women would have the right to decide on whether to terminate a pregnancy, while the ethics of abortion would be contested in families and religious institutions but not through legislative or legal action. But this equilibrium proved to be anything but stable, especially in the United States where abortion rights have become highly politicized and are an ongoing source of polarization, legal battles, and legislative combat. Interestingly, increases and decreases in the actual rates of abortion seem to stem from factors that are largely unrelated to the politics of abortion. Instead, the use of abortion seems correlated to overall fertility rates, improvements in and accessibility to birth control technology, and economic trends (Jones et al. 2019; Blystead et al. 2020). Nonetheless, the conflict remains intense, the stakes high, and no end seems in sight.

Virtually all of us have had some involvement with the issue, whether knowing people or having ourselves chosen to have an abortion (or decided against doing so), being an advocate, participating in heated discussions, dealing with it as teachers, friends, family members, or even as mediators. Finding language that allows different sides to even raise the issue in a constructive way is strikingly difficult. For example, abortion rights advocates do not accept "pro-life" as a fair characterization of abortion opponents and opponents do not accept "pro-choice" as a reasonable description of abortion rights supporters.

We can begin to unpack the nature of long-term, intractable conflicts by considering six different but interrelated elements. (Note: The "Faces of Conflict" were previously discussed in *Staying with Conflict*, Mayer 2009.) Which of these we focus on as interveners, activists, or policymakers has enormous strategic implications, but we often remain unaware of the choices we are making about this. Let's consider the reproductive rights debate through this lens.

- *Low-impact conflict:* Not all elements of even the most polarized conflict have the same impact, even though it's sometimes hard to recognize this in the heat of the struggle. There are often resolvable aspects of a conflict that do not require delving into more fundamental differences and that in themselves do not have profound social or personal impacts. For example, issues regarding abortion clinic names, signs, location, parking arrangements, or advertising are relatively less important than whether abortion should be legal and under what circumstances. But, of course, each of these seemingly lower impact issues become contentious when linked to higher-stakes elements of conflict.

- *Representative conflict:* Every element of a conflict to some extent represents every other element. How we refer to pro-choice and pro-life groups represents our entire narrative of the conflict. Clinic location is hard to separate from whether there ought to be a clinic at all. One of the arts of political organizing is to identify demands that are achievable and ostensibly entirely reasonable but that represent more basic concerns around which a movement might be built.

- *Latent conflict:* Latent conflicts have not yet emerged into the open even though the conditions exist for them to do so. For example, as medical technology improves the availability of non-surgical abortions, a new arena for conflict is likely to emerge (and in some places already has). Sometimes it takes a precipitating event to bring an issue to the fore (such as a dramatic case about the consequences of a teenager being denied access to a medical abortion after a rape), but sometimes a conflict simply matures to the point where it becomes manifest. Identifying latent conflicts and intervening early to either prevent them from erupting or guide how they emerge is an opportunity for interveners and activists.

- *Resolvable conflict:* These are the elements amenable to resolution. Is there any agreement that would once and for all settle the divide on reproductive rights? Probably not. But agreements about providing healthcare services to pregnant teens might be achievable.

- *Stubborn conflict:* This is a potentially resolvable but difficult conflict. Rules for picketing around abortion clinics, for example, have been very contentious, but in a variety of locations, a set of standards have been enacted that have seemed to gain acceptance, perhaps grudgingly. Of course, hard-won solutions that have seemed to resolve a stubborn area of conflict sometimes unravel, such as what appears to be happening with regard to voting rights. This potential always exists because of the connection to the sixth face of conflict:

- *Enduring conflict:* This element won't be resolved, and resolution can't even be clearly imagined because the issue is deeply rooted in our values, the structures we have created, entrenched patterns of power, and the narratives we cling to because they are a source of our identity. We need to delve further into enduring conflict to gain a fuller understanding of the most daunting challenges activists and conflict interveners face.

Enduring Conflict

Consider the most significant conflicts we face in our communities, workplaces, society, or families. Then consider whether you can imagine an agreement that would resolve these conflicts. Enduring conflicts do end, but they require people to evolve and systems to change to do so. Why is it that polarization relating to party politics was a grave concern to George Washington and remains so today? Why have issues of race-based inequality and racial stereotyping been prevalent throughout our history? Why have there been conflicts about the distribution of wealth, immigration, or the rights of individuals versus the power of the state going back centuries? Clearly they are baked into the complexity of the societies we have created and into the contradictory needs we experience as individuals who live in groups. Enduring conflicts tend to exhibit these common characteristics:

- They are embedded in systems that are essential to society's functioning such as governmental, educational, economic, political, safety, healthcare, and infrastructure.

- They have deep historical roots.

- They involve our sense of who we are, our identity.

- They are perpetuated by the narratives we create and that are reflected in the popular culture that reinforces our identity.

- They involve issues of power and power inequities.

- They are complex and interrelated with other enduring conflicts.

- They are value laden.

- They threaten people's sense of security and at times their survival.

Look at the most troublesome conflicts we face and the social movements that are connected to them, and consider how they stack up against these elements—for example, White supremacy and antiracism, misogyny and feminism, or capitalism and workers' rights. The operation of these characteristics explains a great deal about the nature of each struggle. For example, when we consider climate change and the environmental movement:

- Global warming derives from every aspect of what we do and how we live—the economy we have built, our modes of transportation, our dependence on energy and heavy metals, and population growth. The foremost challenge in creating a more sustainable global society is narrowing our focus enough to even name the problem without making it seem as if we are doomed.

- The roots of climate change go back at least to the beginning of the Industrial Age in the late 18th, early 19th century, but some would argue that its sources are even deeper—in our history of urbanization and in agricultural practices that date back centuries. However, these problems have escalated significantly with the dramatic increase in our reliance on fossil fuels and automobiles in the last century.

- To deal with climate change, we need to alter our relationship to what we eat, how we get around, where we live, and our insistence on our individual rights at the expense of the communal good, and all of this is dramatically wrapped up with our sense of who we are.

- Think of how the romance of the road, the travel adventure, and the image of rugged individualism pervade US culture—music, movies, art, and literature. Many people from the United States feel that they have "conquered the frontier," "built a global community," and "produced the most productive economy in history," and each of these accomplishments that are so central to their identity has dramatically contributed to the problems the nation faces.

Transient Movements and Enduring Conflict

All significant movements for social change run up against the challenge of enduring conflict, and therefore they need a strategic approach to their sustainability. They have to adapt their structure, policies, and ideology to evolving circumstances. The lifespan of many social change efforts and the organizations involved with them are frequently shorter than that of the conflict they are addressing. Just because a particular social change effort is short-lived, however, does not mean that it is insignificant over the longer term. Whether it is or not depends on how well its immediate efforts are connected to the enduring nature of the problem.

For example, there have been no less than four waves of feminism and still counting, dating back at least to 1848 when the movement for women's rights and particularly suffrage first came to prominence in the United States at the Seneca Falls Convention. And of course the struggle for equality for women continues.

The anti-war movements of the 1960s and 1970s wound down with the end of the Vietnam War, although the United States' involvement in overseas military actions has never ceased. But the anti–Vietnam War movement can be understood as a particular manifestation of a longer-term struggle against imperialism, colonialism, and militarism.

These efforts were an important part of ongoing struggles but also limited in their vision and politics. Each was a product of its time, each contributed to a developing consciousness, each served as a building block for successive movements for change, and each has been rightly critiqued by them for their limited vision and compromised histories. Confronting those histories is essential to the sustainability of social movements, and doing so can be both painful and liberating.

When we look back at some of the deeply troubling beliefs and behaviors characteristic of the movements out of which current efforts at social change have developed, we may find ourselves embarking on a journey through cognitive dissonance. Abolitionists were racists. Early feminist efforts were about White women. The anti–Vietnam War movement was at times deeply sexist. John Muir, the founder of the Sierra Club, and Margaret Sanger, the founder of Planned Parenthood, were supporters of eugenics, a racist movement that encouraged the forced sterilization of those who were "unfit." Both allied with racists in support of the causes that were important to them, and both supported policies that were harmful to people of color and Indigenous peoples. However, both made important, lasting contributions to progressive causes as well.

The Sierra Club and Planned Parenthood have had to confront their racist pasts (Brune 2020; Johnson 2021). Alexis McGill Johnson, the president of the Planned Parenthood Federation of America, wrote this in a guest opinion in *The New York Times*:

> "We don't know what was in Sanger's heart, and we don't need to in order to condemn her harmful choices.

What we have is a history of focusing on White womanhood relentlessly. Whether our founder was a racist is not a simple yes or no question. Our reckoning is understanding her full legacy, and its impact. Our reckoning is the work that comes next.

"Sanger remains an influential part of our history and will not be erased, but as we tell the history of Planned Parenthood's founding, we must fully take responsibility for the harm that Sanger caused to generations of people with disabilities and Black, Latino, Asian-American, and Indigenous people."

(Johnson, Alexis McGill, "I'm the Head of Planned Parenthood. We're Done Making Excuses for Our Founder," *The New York Times* (online), April 17, 2021])

The willingness of organizations to confront and reject their past shortcomings while embracing the values and commitment to progressive change that are also part of their histories is both a moral imperative and essential to their sustainability as effective agents of social change.

Strategies for Enduring Conflict I: Confronting Avoidance

We are all conflict avoiders at times. Sometimes we have to be in order to exist in groups. We all have to find our way through difficult interactions with family members, friends, neighbors, and colleagues without confronting every instance of tension or disagreement. On the other hand, if we never confront the issues or concerns that we find problematic, or respond to the direct or indirect expressions of others' discomfort with us, we build walls between us, and we allow what might be minor problems to fester into larger ones. And we may be enabling discriminatory power relationships to go unchallenged. We are constantly navigating between engaging and avoiding. When a circumstance abounds with conflicts that are largely ignored or expressed in indirect, passive-aggressive ways, we may find that we are maintaining our connections but at a great cost to ourselves and to the relationships themselves. That is why extended family gatherings, which can be sources of great joy, are often fraught with tension and sadness.

Our avoidant tendencies in interpersonal interactions play out on the large scale of social conflict as well, often through the multitude of individual interactions that are the building blocks of large-scale conflict.

As individuals and as groups we are endlessly creative in how we avoid conflict. For example:

- *We change the subject.* "The issue is not racism but how we learn to communicate better." Or "The problem is cancel culture."

- *We deny.* "I am the least racist person you will ever meet."

- *We minimize.* "We were just joking, just locker-room talk." "The problem is just a few bad cops."

- *We offer premature solutions.* "We are forming a working group to reform police training."

- *We perform.* "I want to honor all those who have suffered from racist policing."

- *We apologize.* "I said I'm sorry. I really am. Now can we move on?"

- *We escalate.* "If you can't take the heat, get out of the kitchen."

Of course we should honor those who have suffered and apologize when appropriate. And as discussed throughout this book, escalating conflict is often essential for promoting social change. But there is a difference between problem-solving to promote a long-term change process and using it to prevent others from raising their most essential concerns or from working on the systemic roots of conflict. Similarly, escalating to prevent an issue from being swept under the table is the opposite of escalating in order to avoid engaging with the issue.

One of the subtlest but most prevalent ways of avoiding conflict, one which we are probably all guilty of on occasion, is *avoidance through performance*. We can wear Black Lives Matter buttons or paint slogans on our basketball courts, or honor the Indigenous owners of the land on which we have built our cities. In themselves, these actions are not inappropriate, but there is an element of virtue-signaling in them, an attempt to let ourselves off the hook by telling the world how anti-racist and clued in we are and thereby avoiding an examination of our own privilege and the way we maintain it.

Confronting Bigotry

Imagine that you are part of a group enjoying a Friday after-work brew at your favorite watering hole. Your connections range from close to casual, and this little gathering has become a standard way of shedding the stresses of your work week. As you engage in the typical and often banal banter that characterizes this time, a long-standing participant says, "I am so pissed off that every time a Black person applies for a job in my company, they get hired, regardless of how incompetent they are, and then everyone is afraid to question this because they don't want to be called a racist." What do you do?

You could say:

- Nothing.

- "Tell me more. What specifically has happened?"

- "Sorry to say this, but you really are being a racist."

- "Hold on, the real problem has been a pattern of historical discrimination."

- "What did you think about that heat wave in British Columbia?"

There may be no perfect answer here, but the initial statement crosses a boundary that calls for a response, ideally one that gives expression to your values, that makes it clear you are not okay with what was just said, and that challenges the stereotyping but also that does not back the person into a corner. Of course, you might end up damaging the relationship and the group's cohesiveness or isolating yourself. No matter how close we may feel to the people involved, it can be remarkably challenging and even frightening to simply say, "That statement seems steeped with racist assumptions."

It is not easy to figure out how to confront racism on an interpersonal level. And our own backgrounds obviously make an enormous difference in how we do it. How Bernie, as an older White male, or Jackie, as a Puerto Rican woman, might experience this interaction and respond to it are likely to be widely different from each other and from the response of a Black person, for example. The negative consequences for making the statement also vary significantly. No matter who we are, though, we still face the dilemma of how to be true to ourselves and our values, how to overcome the avoidant tendencies we might feel, and how to address this in a way that connects to both the interpersonal and social issues involved. And hopefully we can do in a way that honors our friendships if possible.

Of course some interactions are so toxic that avoidance or cutting off the relationship may be the most appropriate response. But if we are open to the possibility that most people can change and express our truths with authenticity, clarity, and humility, we will sometimes be surprised by the change that can occur. Enduring conflict is not the same as unending conflict. People evolve, and that is one important way that system change occurs. They do so for many reasons, but interactions that challenge established narratives and stereotypes are one important impetus.

One impediment to confronting bigotry in all its many guises is that we have developed a set of social norms that make it almost impossible to confront or even just ask one another about our prejudices without creating a defensive reaction. This seems to be especially true about challenging racist actions and beliefs. Labeling something as racist is unfortunately widely seen as particularly toxic. We haven't been able to accept that being called out for racism especially but bigotry more generally does not mean we are evil nor do we have to reject the entire value system and personality of someone we call out. Ibram Kendi distinguishes between talking about what people do and who they are:

> "'Racist' is not . . . a pejorative. It is not the worst word in the English language; it is not the equivalent of a slur. It is descriptive, and the only way to undo racism is to consistently identify and describe it—and then dismantle it. The attempt to turn this usefully descriptive term into an almost unusable slur, is of course, designed to do the opposite: to freeze us into inaction."
>
> (Kendi, *How to Be an Antiracist*
> [New York: One World, 2019], 9)

Of course, the usefulness of trying to go beyond calling out racism and trying to engage with someone depends on what they have done, how willing they are to engage, to reflect, and to change, how dangerous their actions have been, and what the power dimensions of our relationships are. It's not as simple as saying, if everyone just learns to communicate better, we can all get along. But it is critical to look at what makes it so hard to raise fundamental issues of oppression and privilege, to grasp how important it is to do this, and to face how easily we avoid it.

Calling Out and Cancel Culture

The boundary between necessary escalation and avoidant escalation is sometimes nonexistent. "Cancel culture" provides an interesting example of this. How, for example, can we confront sexist behavior, language, or attitudes without dooming the chances of communicating with people who might be willing to learn from the confrontation?

The term "cancel culture" oversimplifies the issue and assumes that any effort to hold people accountable for egregious behavior in a public manner is extremist. It also implies, completely without justification, that "canceling" someone is a phenomenon characteristic only of progressive movements (think about the right-wing reaction to Republican officials who upheld the US election results in 2020). What falls under the rubric of cancel culture includes both a constructive but firm calling out of dangerous behavior and the narratives that justify them as well as a public ganging up on someone who has made a minor transgression in a way that seeks to destroy them and all those who associate with them.

What has come to be called cancel culture is an increased willingness of victims of racism and misogyny and their allies to publicly let someone or some entity know that racist or misogynist statements or actions are unacceptable and hurtful, that is, to call them out. The term "cancel culture" has become a pejorative label used to dismiss and discourage people from calling out behavior, even when it is important and effective to do so. The criticisms of cancel culture are almost always an effort to dismiss the seriousness of individual actions or the prevalence of systemic sources of oppression. Calling out is a critical tool for interrupting harm or hitting a quick pause on a toxic interaction. Moreover, it is a means of changing a culture that allows and reinforces racist and misogynist behavior to one that challenges these actions and is characterized by a heightened sensitivity to the significant harm they cause.

If we are called out, instead of being defensive, we may want to ask ourselves what in our comments or attitude has compelled someone to call us out. To be sure, as with almost any tool for confronting oppression, calling out can be overused and overdone, but it is an important tool that we all need to learn to use and to respond to effectively. "Calling in," on the other hand, is an invitation to explore and learn together. Rather than being confrontational, calling in invokes a curious stance as to why a comment was made or an action taken and invites a conversation that leads to a deeper understanding. Such a conversation will only be effective if people feel psychologically safe. The goal of calling out in a sense is to set the stage for calling in.

Ezra Klein discussed the need for public shaming (which is his description of cancel culture) along with the danger of engaging in it:

> "Too few people have decided the boundaries of unacceptable speech for too long, and part of what we're going through now is an important renegotiation of that. That renegotiation will just have to take place through social means, including shame. There's no other way to do it. It is not something you can just do with a piece of legislation, but I do worry that online discourse is so tuned to shaming that we've lost sight of some of its drawbacks. Shaming people, it makes them defensive. It makes them into enemies rather than helping them become allies, and then we think too little about other virtues and skills which [we need to] develop to be good political or even just human communicators."
>
> (Klein, "Transcript: Ezra Klein Interviews Natalie Wynn and Will Wilkinson" [*The Ezra Klein Show*, NYTimes.com, April 27, 2021])

We might not always be able to walk the fine line between calling out behavior and cancelling the person, and maybe social change activists in particular should not be expected to take this on as their responsibility. Maybe their task is to raise the issue in a powerful way and thereby provoke a different type of interchange. And yet, finding opportunities to have authentic interchanges with those who are open to looking at themselves is a powerful part of how attitudes change. We certainly saw that in the change in attitudes toward marriage equality, for example.

We are always avoiding conflict, and we are always in conflict somewhere in our lives. Figuring out how to raise conflicts effectively, over time, in a sustainable way is a core element in the strategic disruption of oppressive systems. Another dimension of this is developing our ability to respond appropriately when others raise difficult issues with us and learning to respond in an honest and non-defensive way, even when an issue has not been raised in a particularly constructive way. This requires that we learn to listen first, own what we ought to own, apologize when apologies are warranted, raise concerns we might have in return, and see such moments as opportunities for personal growth and relationship building. This too is central to our capacity to have genuine and rewarding human interactions.

Strategies for Enduring Conflict II: The Use of Representative Conflict

Every social movement focuses on issues that are immediate, tangible, and on which progress is possible in building for long-term change. These efforts are most effective when they tie the immediate and sometimes short-lived experience of oppression to the systemic issues they represent. When movements fail to do this and instead focus solely on the transient elements of a conflict, significant as these may be, they become more vulnerable not only to the failure of their efforts but to their successes.

The feminist movement in the United States put considerable energy and resources into passing the Equal Rights Amendment in the 1970s. The failure of this effort was very dispiriting and sapped energy from the overall efforts to advance gender equality. The anti-war movement of the same era was successful, but its success led to the retreat of a strong progressive movement, a retreat that lasted over 30 years. Of course, there were many other reasons for this, but the weakness of the connections established between the transient and enduring aspects of conflict was significant.

Electoral campaigns sometimes help to build movements but are also frequently a distraction from the long-term focus movements need. Progressives in the United States put a great deal of effort into the presidential campaigns of Robert Kennedy, Eugene McCarthy, George McGovern, Jesse Jackson, Ralph Nader, and others. In England, similar hope was put into the former Labor Party leader Jeremy Corbyn. But electoral politics is stacked against genuine change efforts, and on the whole these campaigns led to disappointment and a dissipation of both focus and energy. On the other hand, strong social movements have leveraged political candidates to adopt policies that furthered their goals, such as the increased attention to climate change in Europe and North America.

That's not to say that movements should only focus on the long term. That is not an effective or realistic approach. And choosing the right issue to focus on is certainly not a science. Furthermore, figuring out the right way to maintain the connection between the transient and the enduring is seldom obvious. But when movements accomplish this linkage, their effectiveness is almost always enhanced.

Example: The Campaign Against NDAs

Consider the current effort to change a practice that has enabled sexual abuse to proliferate, that is clearly connected to the long-term problem of abuse and assault, but that is a very specific and immediate issue that provides a tangible and practical target—namely the use of nondisclosure agreements (NDAs) when dealing with sexual misconduct.

How is it possible that sexual (and other) abuse has proliferated—and continues—in so many institutions despite professed commitments to ending it? From the Catholic and Anglican Churches to the US Olympic Committee, from universities to the military and police departments, from schools to residential facilities for at-risk youth and adults, the failure of institutions everywhere to protect the vulnerable and hold the powerful accountable is astounding. Even though the ongoing revelations of horrific abuse have tarnished the reputations of these institutions and enormous amounts of money have been spent on legal defense and settlements, sexual assault and other abusive practices have continued. Why?

Many institutions are more concerned about protecting their privileged status than adhering to their ostensible mission, and therefore they focus on safeguarding those in power who in turn deliver rewards or consequences to others. One way this is accomplished is to isolate the incidents of misconduct so that a systemic pattern is never acknowledged or confronted. Abusive behaviors by particular individuals are minimized and isolated. When victims or their advocates raise an issue of assault or abuse, the initial response of the institutional authorities is to question, to minimize, and to threaten the reporter. Victims of rape who report their abuse to police, for example, are routinely questioned, ignored, delayed, blamed, and re-traumatized.

When reports are taken seriously and the initial denials or counterattacks from perpetrators are resisted, and even when a finding is made that abuse has occurred, the abuse is treated as confidential and victims are pressured, sometimes forced, into signing nondisclosure agreements. NDAs and institutional enabling are what allowed Bill Cosby, Donald Trump, Larry Nasser, and Harvey Weinstein to continue to abuse those vulnerable to their power and status.

Of course, these celebrity cases are just the very tip of the iceberg. Every day, victims of abuse are offered financial compensation in return for signing NDAs. Moreover, they are often subjected to considerable pressure, sometimes by their own lawyers, to agree to maintain secrecy as a means of "bringing closure to their case." Educational institutions, corporations, and government agencies that dismiss employees whom they have determined to be perpetrators agree to NDAs with those whose employment is being terminated to prevent reputational damage and forestall litigation.

These NDAs cause significant damage. For one thing, they do not achieve closure for victims who are prevented from speaking up about their experiences, sometimes even to family members or therapists. If they have left an organization due to its hostile environment, they are prevented from telling future employers why they left, leaving a hole in their employment history that they cannot explain. Furthermore, NDAs endanger the public by allowing perpetrators to hide their past as they seek new positions in which they can continue to prey on vulnerable targets.

Zelda Perkins was one of many people who signed an NDA with Harvey Weinstein and was the first to break it when she realized how many other people had been abused by him. In an interview with *The Guardian*, she explains her motivation:

> "'[NDAs] were designed for protection of intellectual property, or if two people want to make a consensual agreement not to have an argument dealt with publicly,' says Perkins. 'There is nothing ethical about a legal agreement that hides damaging behaviour—bullying, racism, any form of assault—[and] protects that kind of information and works purely for the powerful. The disparity of power in nearly every situation an NDA is used is shocking.'
>
> Weinstein, she says, was a distraction from the real problem—the system in which he operated, including

the use of NDAs—and she is determined that, now he is in prison, the issue will not go away. 'There are always going to be Harveys, but if the law doesn't protect you, then we're screwed. I didn't have power over Harvey, I didn't have power over the case, but what I can do is try to change the system that enables men like him.'

(Perkins on NDAs from Saner, "Interview: Zelda Perkins: 'There will always be men like Weinstein. All I can do is try to change the system that enables them'" [*The Guardian*, December 23, 2020])

The use of NDAs has come under attack by activists in the #MeToo movement and elsewhere, and several jurisdictions have now passed or are considering legislation to ban NDAs to cover up sexual and other harassment. (For more on NDAs, see Macfarlane 2020 and https://cantbuymysilence.com/.)

The use of NDAs is a powerful example of how the right issue can become the rallying cry and focal point for an effort to attack a deeply systemic problem. It meets three key criteria for connecting a transient conflict with an enduring and systemic one:

- The immediate problem is tangible, understandable, and galvanizing.

- Its connection with the systemic issue is unmistakable and revealing.

- Progress can be made on the transient conflict in a way that reinforces efforts to build a movement for systemic change.

The Power of "Transitional" Issues

Other examples of transitional issues (such as NDAs) include:

- The Keystone Pipeline
- Stop-and-search policing policies

- Prison reform

- Voting rights

- Hurricane relief for Puerto Rico

The potential of each of these to both attack an immediate problem and galvanize a movement for change depends on the organization, timing, leadership, and strategy involved. Consider, for example, the "Defund the Police" slogan and movement. This has been a powerful focal point for protests against police misconduct but more than that, a direct attack against the system behind that conduct. The problem is tangible and galvanizing, its connection to systemic racism unmistakable. But this focus has been criticized by many as being divisive and providing an excellent target for those who want to discredit efforts to reform policing. And it is unlikely to happen.

However, just because this focus goes too far for some (e.g. President Biden) does not negate its effectiveness as a rallying call. It clearly expresses the deep frustration of those who feel targeted by police and who fear for their children's safety. The slogan goes straight to the systemic roots of the issue and expresses feelings and beliefs that many in power would like to ignore or suppress. Transitional issues and the slogans that define them are rarely perfect and evolve as a movement evolves. If they don't somehow upset those in power, then they are likely missing something important.

When progress is made on immediate issues, there is cause to rejoice (as when Derek Chauvin was convicted of George Floyd's murder or when the Keystone Pipeline was cancelled). We need to be able to celebrate tangible achievements. But at the same time, we need to use victories as an opportunity to connect to the larger issues and to solidify commitments to an ongoing struggle. Philonise Floyd (George Floyd's brother) made these powerful connections after the verdict in the Chauvin trial:

"Just listening to those words, guilty, and guilty, and guilty on all counts, that was a moment that I will never be able to relive—I will always have it inside of me. It's just being able to note that it's justice for African American People, justice for people of color, period, in this world. This is monumental. This is historic. This is a pivotal moment in history, and all I can think about is Emmett Till, I think about Sandra Bland, I think about Miss Carr [Eric Garner's mother, Gwen Carr], Eric Garner. It's so many people we have known being killed: Daunte Wright, I think about Jacob Blake, I think about Philando Castile. All of these people, they are all dead. . . . We all need justice, and we're all fighting for one reason and it's justice for all. And I think today has been an occasion where people can celebrate. But tomorrow it's back to business, because we have to stay steps ahead of everything, and we'll keep pushing, and we'll keep pushing, and . . . we'll keep fighting. . . . We will cement his legacy forever all around the word. Because if you can make federal laws to protect . . . the bald eagle, you can make federal laws to protect people of color."

(Philonise Floyd, "George Floyd's brother reacts to Chauvin Guilty verdict" [CNN *Interview*, April 20, 2021])

Strategies for Enduring Conflict III: Durable Communication and Sustainable Power

Conflict interveners dealing with enduring conflict have to consider not only immediate communication challenges but how to build durable systems of communication. For activists, the bigger challenge may be how to move from a focus on immediate power struggles to a strategic consideration of how to build a movement's power over time.

Durable Communication

For divorcing parents, the communication challenge is sometimes intense. There are circumstances where all direct communication must cease, but unless domestic violence is involved, it is usually essential to find a way to communicate that does not stir up volatile conflict or catch the children in the middle of parental disagreements. Easier said than done if the divorce is bitter and anger levels intense. Several elements need to be present to sustain effective communication in the face of ongoing tensions and disagreements. These include:

- Recognition by all parties that maintaining some form of communication is necessary and that the ongoing co-parenting relationship is important;

- Clear parameters and boundaries;

- Multiple realistic channels and modes for communicating;

- Feedback systems about what is working and what isn't (sometimes this necessitates third parties, coaches, or advocates);

- Commitment to guidelines for keeping children out of the middle;

- Time-out procedures (when a break is necessary, hopefully before destructive interactions have gotten out of hand).

These elements are intended to assist in creating a sustainable system of communication, especially when things get rough. They are not the same as good communication practices more generally—such as effective listening, truth telling, framing, and feedback, although those are important as well. With some adaptations, we can apply these standards to enduring conflicts in communities, organizations, and social networks. Consider, for example, a not uncommon ongoing conflict between an environmental advocacy group in a small town and a consortium of corporate agricultural interests.

Burton is a small town with a split identity. It is blessed with a pleasant climate, rich farmland, and a scenic location that has long attracted campers, fishers, and birdwatchers. Historically it has serviced medium-sized family farms, orchards, and dairy farms. More recently corporate farming has expanded rapidly, which has led to clearing many orchards, erecting large-scale structures, employing water- and energy-intensive practices, and relying on seasonal laborers, many of whom are migrant workers. At the same time Burton has also experienced a growth in tourism, vacation home ownership, restaurants, microbreweries, and boutique stores.

While there has been tension between agricultural and tourist interests for a long time, these new developments have exacerbated these differences. Town council elections and meetings have become struggles between those advocating for growth and those promoting policies to protect the environment and maintain the "elegant, small-town charm" of Burton. Some specific issues have brought these differences to the fore—the increasing toll of agricultural waste on the watershed, an outbreak of COVID-19 among seasonal workers, a significant increase in trucking traffic, and a proposal to build a large upscale housing development on open space adjacent to town. Specific agreements have been

(Continued)

(*Continued*)

reached to control trucking traffic through town, to require a certain amount of open space to be included in new development plans, and to provide medical services for seasonal workers, but the split identity of the town suggests that the overall conflict will not readily disappear.

This scenario is an amalgam of situations the two of us have dealt with in a number of locations. Agreements on specific issues are often possible, but their long-term effectiveness depends on the ability of different groups to continue to communicate even as they build support for their interests and occasionally vilify each other. Let's consider how the elements applied to a family conflict might apply to Burton.

- *Do the multiple different interests recognize that some form of ongoing communication is important?* The town will continue to have to make decisions that pit the different groups against each other. Long-term residents will want to see the economy grow and to preserve the nature of their town. They will likely have friends and relatives working in both the tourist and agricultural sectors. New residents, for example, retirees from urban centers or wealthy families purchasing second homes, may prove to be essential allies for a variety of interest groups, but they also may be resented by many in these groups as well. Communication among political leaders and proponents of different interests will occur one way or another—even if just through opposing statements at city council meetings, social media activity, or legal action. The question, therefore, is whether the need to communicate directly is acknowledged and whether the procedures for doing so are established.

- *Are there parameters to communicating about differences that should be honored?* Key players may be neighbors, work out at the same gym, have kids in schools together, or be members of the same church. Should there be de facto or overt limits on how they communicate when they run into each other in community settings? What about how they interact on social media?

- *Are there multiple enduring channels of communication?* If the only communication is through social media or in legal settings, then their most polarizing differences are likely to be the ongoing focus. Just as there need to be parameters, there need to be a variety of mechanisms for differences to be discussed, understanding to be increased, and relevant agreements to be sought.

- *Do feedback systems exist?* Can agricultural representatives and environmentalists communicate that a particular demand or proposal is likely to exacerbate differences, perhaps unnecessarily? For example, if an environmentalist is asking that all large trucks be forbidden from traveling through the core of the town at all times, effectively putting certain agricultural facilities out of business, is there a means by which the potential consequences of this proposal can be communicated directly? More generally, is there a way of exploring which issues might be resolvable, who might be amenable to discussing them, and what degree of confidentiality would be necessary to do so? This type of feedback is where the use of an intermediary might be particularly useful, so a related question to this (and the previous one) is what formal and informal third-party resources are available?

- *Are children involved?* Children might actually be involved (they go to school together, are friends, etc.), but there are analogies to children—institutions or service providers who ought to be kept out of the direct conflict such as educational leaders, healthcare providers, fire or police officers, or seasonal workers.

- *Will there be times when direct and indirect communication cannot be constructive?* Are there ways of taking a break from this, signaling the need to do so, and returning to direct communication when ready? Are there ground rules to maintain during such a break?

- *Are we encouraging the participants to reimagine and redefine their relationships?* Are we supporting a shift from a transactional communication process toward a relationship-based one?

In a small community or organization, there is often a strong incentive, even in the face of extreme differences, to maintain some kind of communication among conflicting groups. The larger the system, the more likely it is that there will be at least some groups or individuals who understand their role to be primarily to articulate differences, disrupt systems, and organize movements (or to fight against movements for change). Even in these circumstances, some system of interaction is likely to exist. Sometimes, as previously suggested, this occurs through different advocacy organizations playing different roles. But even when groups are focused on disruptive activities and drawing a strong moral contrast to those representing opposing interests, some sort of system of communication with their opposition is almost always necessary. This is a setting where the work of conflict interveners and activists is often synergetic.

For example, when I (Bernie) was involved in organizing demonstrations against the Rocky Flats Nuclear Weapons Plant in Colorado in the late 1970s and early 1980s, I was impressed that even when there were ongoing sit-ins and multiple arrests occurring on the tracks that led into the plant, there were always some mechanisms for the demonstrators to communicate with plant security officials and local law enforcement. The sit-ins went on for almost two years, and there were ongoing demonstrations, including a mass encirclement of the plant, that went on for years after that (the plant closed in 1992). These channels of communication were maintained throughout. (We will discuss the series of actions at Rocky Flats further in Chapters 7 and 9.)

Sustainable Power

Building a social movement is about building social power, and activists have to determine how to gather power, how to employ it intentionally and effectively, how to share it, and how to sustain and grow it. Our power as individuals and groups is always interactive, context dependent, and dynamic. What works well is dependent on the circumstances it is employed in, the response of others, and our response to their response.

The most effective strategy for developing sustainable power is not necessarily the best approach to rally initial support for a movement for change. We distinguish chaotic disruption from strategic disruption to identify spontaneous actions that are often a result of anger in reaction to immediate events versus planned and deliberate efforts to create a sustained campaign to disrupt entrenched systems.

In recent times, police violence has provoked clear and dramatic spontaneous responses to the death of people of color at the hands of law enforcement. However, almost immediately activists sought to channel the spontaneous energy of this chaotic effort at disruption into more sustainable approaches to exerting power over time. This transition is seldom smooth, the boundaries between chaotic and strategic disruption are unclear and porous, and the reactions of those in power often provoke further chaotic responses. Officials are prone to respond to demonstrations harshly (with tear gas, tasers, water hoses, etc.), resulting in injuries and widespread arrests. These in turn provoke more spontaneous outpourings of anger, thus creating an escalating and chaotic cycle. Efforts to channel the response in a more sustainable way continue and over time may prevail—until the next extreme (sometimes intentional) provocation occurs. (For a timeline of the protests and reactions to George Floyd's murder, see Taylor 2021).

One specific example of how this channeling occurred has taken place at the intersection of East 38th Street and Chicago Avenue in Minneapolis, the location of George Floyd's murder. Initially the site of spontaneous protests, it has gradually evolved into a focus for community gathering and ongoing activism. And it has also become a place of pilgrimage for those who want to honor and remember Floyd. A small garden has been erected at the precise location of Floyd's murder. The location has been renamed (unofficially so far) George Floyd Square. Community and religious leaders have participated in events there, calling for ongoing peaceful protests. The occupation remains illegal, although negotiations are ongoing as to the future of the site.

The effort to assert sustainable power is generally characterized by:

- The emergence of both formal and informal leadership;

- The participation of community organizations (e.g. religious, political, educational);

- Attention to the public message that actions convey and the means of doing so;

- Creation of a structure for decision making, recruitment, and resource development, which often means creating new organizations or repurposing existing ones;

- Establishing means of communication—formal and informal

- Negotiations of some sort with the "powers that be";

- The articulation of a strategy for change, including a clear set of proposals.

The goal is to develop the movement for change and to develop a strategy to respond to the likely pushback from authorities. A dilemma activists face is that the more organized a process becomes, the less threatening to the establishment and therefore the easier to resist, ignore, or co-opt. But a totally disorganized or chaotic response is harder to maintain and will eventually dissipate, and the reaction of those in power to these is to try to control and to stall. There is a symbiotic relationship between spontaneous and planned disruption. The power of nonviolence as a strategy for change lies in its capacity to harness the tension between chaotic and strategic approaches to change. We return to a discussion of this dynamic in Chapter 7.

Sustaining Ourselves in Enduring Conflict

"If I can't dance, I don't want to be part of your revolution."

—Emma Goldman (attributed)

Long-term engagement in conflict or in social change efforts can be both energizing and exhausting. Our participation in these can give us a sense of purpose and connection with others, but it also can burn us out, especially as we contend with all the other demands of our lives. Finding ways to sustain ourselves and those we are working with is critical to the success of long-term change efforts. We know that it requires allies to work with, but also a network of supporters with whom we can share our experiences, exchange advice, trade stories, complain and rejoice, and offer emotional support. Often, we need help in developing the financial resources to allow us to continue to focus on a change effort.

We also need safe havens, the people and spaces that allow us to escape from the stress, danger, and intensity of social change efforts. We all need to live a life that is not entirely about conflict or social change even if that is what we have dedicated our lives to. We each need our own version of dancing (which may be dancing). We may find this in our families, in recreational activities, in music or art, in unrelated work that is meaningful to us, in religious activities, or in meditation. We should not look on these as distractions from our "real work" but as an essential part of it.

Social action should be life-giving to us, and we need to build the support systems that help make it so. We each have to find our own path to this, but we should all be attentive to this need and on the alert for when we or others are burning out. This chapter ends with a reflective dialogue about what has helped sustain the two of us in our work on enduring conflicts and social change efforts.

Reflective Dialogue: Sustaining the Effort

Bernie: When I think of the years I have spent trying to build conflict intervention services and at the same time sustain my commitment to social change, I realize how often the major obstacle has been personal stress. Several things have always helped, close personal relations, exercise, the outdoors, and escape into literature (sometimes pretty crappy literature). When my personal life has felt in turmoil, these have been even more important. What has been the most sustaining for you, Jackie?

Jackie: Without a doubt, close friends and family. Advancing social change is simultaneously exhilarating and overwhelming. It is particularly difficult when people within the system become abusive. Sometimes, your mere presence is perceived as threatening by those who want to sustain an oppressive system. During those times, the support of friends, family, music, and going to my home, Puerto Rico, sustain me. Despite the challenges, I am passionate about advancing social and institutional change. Doing this work, I have made lifetime friends, and some of those friends have become family. I have grown professionally, personally, and spiritually in ways I never expected. I also see a younger generation determined to make a more just world, and that gives me hope and also sustains me. What keeps you going, Bernie?

Bernie: Having a life outside the conflict and relationships independent of it. Also, having a safe, conflict-free space. That I am able to have these is a sign of privilege. Black youth, particularly in large urban areas, don't really have safe spaces, for example, and conflict has a way of pounding down doors. But I suspect many find some equivalent to that, like sports or music, or relatively safe places to hang out. When I was in college, I was part of a student cooperative. This wasn't exactly isolated from the conflicts of the day since many of its members were student activists, but for me it was a place of support and insulation from the emotional intensity all around. I visited this same co-op at the time of my 50th reunion and found that it continues to serve that function to this day. Safe spaces are not just physical locations but groups of people whom we feel we can trust, be our least filtered selves with, and have fun with. Where are your safe spaces?

Jackie: My safe spaces are my affinity groups. When I lived in Omaha, I was part of a group of mostly Puerto Rican friends, and we would get together, eat, party, and dance salsa. It provided a space where we could speak Spanish, eat our traditional food, support each other, and be our authentic

(*Continued*)

(*Continued*)

selves. Strengthening affinity groups enhances our capacity to work for social change. Many times, this is the only space where marginalized people can be empowered and supported as they navigate the oppressive institutions they face every day of their lives.

chapter six

beyond evil, stupid, and crazy: systems of privilege and oppression

"Just when you think you've seen and heard it all from Donald Trump, he sinks to a new low that leaves you speechless and wondering: Is he crazy, is he evil, is he maniacally committed to unwinding every good thing Barack Obama did, or is he just plain stupid?"

—Thomas Friedman

No doubt, many of the readers of this book would like nothing better than to relegate Donald Trump to the "dustbin of history." So would the two of us, but Trump, or at least the system that produced him, is still very much with us. We do not need to understand Trump the man, but we do need to grapple with Trump the phenomenon.

Many of us have struggled with a series of basically unanswerable Trump-related questions since before he was elected: How on earth can people continue to support this corrupt, incompetent, racist, misogynist, homophobic narcissist? How has he managed to dominate so much of our national and international dialogue and consciousness? What can his supporters be thinking (especially in view of his chaotic and lethal response to COVID-19 and his efforts to overthrow American democracy)?

To get our hands around the Trump phenomenon and by extension around the hold that White racism continues to have, we have to move beyond the easy answers (the "crazy, stupid, and evil" ones) and look at the nature of the systems that gave rise to Trump and perpetuate racism.

Many of these questions, or at least the underlying concerns they represent, have been with us for far longer than the Trump circus. No matter where we fall on the political spectrum, we all at times find it hard to fathom how people can continue to stand behind politicians we see as dangerous, incompetent, and immoral. But the tenor of that incredulity varies depending on perspective. There is plenty of outrage among Trump's base, but apparently not that much confusion or disorientation. They seem pretty devoid of the cognitive dissonance that most progressives think is the very least they should experience. In fact, whereas Trump's level of support seems to bring despair to his opponents, his supporters seem to be energized and even overjoyed by the confusion and exasperation they evoke in others.

As discussed throughout this book, a neutral façade is not necessary, helpful, or honest in trying to make sense of deeply entrenched conflict. But we should not let our outrage at the actions of individuals prevent us from considering the forces that potentiate their behavior. We need to enlarge our focus beyond the personality and motives of the individuals involved. Real change requires this. The defenders of established power structures, including those that sustain racism and misogyny, would like nothing more than to direct our understanding of racial or sexual violence toward the characteristics of the individual actors and away from systemic factors. It's not White racist culture or economic structures that are to blame, they argue, but racists. Blame Derek Chauvin, not the policing system in America. And don't even try to understand or teach Critical Race Theory.

Deepening our understanding of the Trump phenomenon won't itself diminish its power but can provide a point of entry into facing our most foundational societal problems. Let's start by accepting that many of us who are committed to social change really don't understand what drives the enduring support that Trump has received. And that is a problem. Not simply because of the need to reach out and connect with those we disagree with but because our lack of understanding is disempowering. If we don't understand the roots of his support, it's hard to act in a strategic and confident manner to challenge the systems behind it.

There has been no shortage of efforts do so (e.g. Bradlee 2018; Lind 2020; Pettigrew 2017). This chapter takes this issue on because it is part of the central challenge all of us who are concerned about social change and constructive conflict engagement face and because it provides a useful introduction to how we can understand in practical terms the nature of systems and how they change.

Three Crutches

To understand where others are coming from, we have to dig past the more superficial explanations we are prone to rely on because they are clear and comforting. In particular, we have to move beyond our reliance on three crutches that we use to make sense of behavior that we don't understand or approve of. These are:

- *The stupid crutch*: People are just too stupid to understand what is really going on. Trump's supporters just don't get it. Fox News, Breitbart, the Drudge Report, Newsmax, and the whole right-wing media/Internet bubble feed their ignorance.

- *The evil crutch:* People lack the moral compass or fiber to act ethically. Trump's supporters are racists, misogynists, and Islamophobes. They don't care about what's right, just what is in it for them. They care about their tribe and no one else.

- *The crazy crutch:* People are out of touch with reality. The behavior of people at Trump's rallies shows signs of mass hysteria and paranoia. Those rallying against wearing masks and for carrying arms in public buildings are crazy. Trump himself has a personality disorder.

We have all used simplistic explanations of this type to try to make sense of actions or beliefs that we find both horrifying and unfathomable. A particularly poignant example of how hard it is to avoid defaulting to these crutches is the various ways in which we try to understand the Holocaust. We view the Nazis as crazy and evil, and their followers as gullible and perhaps not very bright. There was of course plenty of crazy, evil, and stupid going around that was part of the story of the rise of Nazi Germany. But these characteristics are not limited to fascists or the MAGA crowd. They can be found everywhere. So why do they get potentiated at some times and not others? Why was Hitler able to come to power when he did and with the program he proposed when at other times, he would have remained a marginal figure?

Trump's supporters no doubt include some who are unbalanced, sociopathic, or not particularly bright. But so do those supporting candidates across the whole political spectrum. It may be that a populist or radical movement is likely to provide a more welcoming home for people who don't fit in easily into more mainstream movements. But this alone does not explain the participation of the bulk of Trump supporters—or of supporters of other extreme political leaders or movements. And it certainly does not explain why these forces have become so powerful.

Many of us have experienced similar efforts to discount our own political actions in support of causes that we believed were just and righteous:

In the late 1960s, I (Bernie) attended a speech delivered by Bruno Bettelheim, a famous—at times infamous—psychoanalyst and author (Goleman 1990), in which he dismissed the actions of anti-war activists as nothing more than adolescent rebellion. Bettelheim and my father were colleagues—they both were directors of residential treatment centers for children as well as survivors of the Buchenwald concentration camp. On a couple of occasions, he had been to our home for dinner. I didn't exactly know him, but I knew he and my father shared a lot in common. So his dismissal of activism as adolescent rebellion was particularly disturbing to me—and absurd. After his talk I approached him and asked whether he thought it was really that simple, whether our concerns about Vietnam, civil rights, gender equality, and student rights could be dismissed as nothing more than adolescent rebellion. Sure enough, that was exactly what he thought—that we were simply acting out of a need to differentiate ourselves, an analysis which he embellished with some psychoanalytic jargon.

He was not alone. Similar dismissals of the activists of that era could be found in the popular culture and in the responses of universities, political leaders, and of many in our own families. And we did it too. In fact, I (Bernie) continue to think Bettelheim was kind of evil, not as smart as he thought, and maybe a bit off-kilter. Later revelations about how he treated youth and staff at the Orthogenic School in Chicago, which he directed, plagiarism he may have committed, and ways he may have falsified his credentials seemed to confirm that.

But while there is sometimes truth in these attributions (I may have been partially acting out against parental norms), the crazy,

stupid, and evil characterizations are shallow and counterproductive. They don't explain deep-seated conflict. They are examples
of *fundamental attribution error*—explaining behavior on the basis
of disposition or personality rather than on situational or systemic
factors (Allred 2000). And they get in the way of achieving a useful
understanding of the fervor of Trump's supporters (90% approval
rating among Republicans as we write this).

So let's try asking three questions:

- What are the needs, interests, and concerns of Trump
  supporters?

- How does their sense of identity, community, and purpose
  come into play (what are their identity needs)?

- What systemic factors are they responding to (even if they
  don't understand it in this way)?

Needs, Interests, and Concerns

Mediators and negotiators are very familiar with the first question.
It's the bread-and-butter of our everyday lives. Of course Trump
supporters have a wide range of concerns, but some are particularly
broadly held and clearly articulated. Let's look at a couple of these.

The Return of Higher Paying, More Secure Jobs. This has been
translated into wanting a return of manufacturing and coal mining
jobs in particular and became a major issue in the 2016 campaign.
The different responses of Hillary Clinton and Donald Trump are
instructive.

Clinton argued that some jobs are going to be lost, that this is
inevitable given the world we are living in, and offered a plan to
encourage the creation of new jobs with good pay and benefits.
Specifically, in response to a question from a coal miner, Clinton
said, "We're going to make it clear that we don't want to forget
those people. Those people labored in those mines for generations,

losing their health, often losing their lives to turn on our lights and power our factories. Now we've got to move away from coal and all the other fossil fuels, but I don't want to move away from the people who did the best they could to produce the energy that we relied on" (quoted by Horsley 2016).

Her proposed solution was a $30 billion fund, focused especially on Appalachia, to invest in retraining, infrastructure, small business development, and the continuation of healthcare and other benefits for those who have lost jobs due to mine closures.

Trump's response was that he was going to bring manufacturing and coal mining jobs back. For example, he said, "Their jobs have been taken away, and we're going to bring them back, folks. If I get in, this is what it is" (quoted in Hagan 2016).

Guess which approach worked better? Trump defeated Clinton by huge majorities in the coal country of Appalachia. It's very likely that her plan was better designed to address the underlying problems that were leading to the loss of jobs and job security. But Trump promised to bring their jobs back. She did not. Very likely, there was no way he could have done this in mining or manufacturing. But he was more effective in speaking to the concerns of those populations as they experienced them. Throughout his presidency he continued to promise to bring mining and manufacturing jobs back—and in fact claimed that he already had. He also made it clear that he would not let environmental concerns get in the way of his efforts to accomplish this. After Trump's defeat and his failure to make a significant dent in the loss of mining jobs and with the increasingly apparent and seemingly inevitable decline in coal mining, miners' unions began to take a Clinton-type approach more seriously (Krugman 2021).

Stemming the Impact of Immigrants. Another hope of Trump supporters was to stem the loss of jobs due to immigrants and to prevent undesirable immigrants from affecting people's well-being. There is a significant racist and xenophobic element here, but let's avoid the "evil" crutch for a moment (we will shortly explore another dimension of this issue) and take these concerns at face value.

In the face of economic inequality and stress, political leaders and the economic elite have long deflected the anger of the less privileged onto immigrants, minorities, or "others" of some kind. The most prominent and pernicious example in US history is how African Americans were scapegoated for the economic woes of working-class Whites. But we have previously seen the Irish, German, Italians, Chinese, Jews, eastern Europeans, south Asians, and others blamed for economic woes—both by those on the left and the right. More recently, Latinx immigrants have become a primary source of concern. And there is this element of reality behind these concerns. Immigrants and minorities have been forced to accept low paying jobs and miserable working conditions because of their lack of power, paucity of choices, and overall vulnerability. And then they faced scapegoating for undercutting the bargaining power of the White working class. Quite the double bind. But the concerns of many Trump supporters, while often misdirected, are nonetheless real. Well-paying blue-collar jobs, particularly in manufacturing, have decreased and so has the power of the unions that represent these workers. The COVID-19 crisis has exacerbated fear of migrant workers and of Asian Americans (immigrant or not) in particular.

Immigrants have by and large significantly lower crime rates than those born in the United States, and an increase in immigration, legal or illegal, is not associated with higher crime—in fact it may be associated with a decrease in crime (Flagg 2017). However, the fear of immigrations-related crime continues to be widely held. And the fact that illegal immigration is to some extent tolerated by our system, even as it is punished, seems to stimulate a more general sense that the system is rigged (which it is—see below).

How has Trump addressed these interests? In a speech devoted to immigration on August 30, 2016, he stated:

". . . we have to listen to the concerns that working people, our forgotten working people, have over the record pace of immigration and its impact on their jobs, wages, housing, schools, tax bills and general living conditions."

(quoted in Bump, "The Fix" [*The New York Times*, August 31, 2016])

And

"While there are many illegal immigrants in our country who are good people, many, many, this doesn't change the fact that most illegal immigrants are lower skilled workers with less education, who compete directly against vulnerable American workers, and that these illegal workers draw much more out from the system than they can ever possibly pay back."

(ibid.)

Trump has talked about immigration for many years. This speech was perhaps the most important talk he gave about immigration during his first presidential campaign. He is here addressing the interests of his target audience as he and his aides understood them. And it resonated. For better or worse, it still does.

Looking for Interests beneath Interests. When we try to understand what motivates those with whom we disagree, it is important that we try to understand their needs from their own point of view. However, we should not accept without question the first level of interests—the ones that people express most readily—as necessarily being representative of their core concerns. For example, why should people who are concerned about the loss of financial well-being be so averse to alternative programs that might in the long run have a better chance of addressing the employment realities in manufacturing or mining? At least one answer to that has to do with tangibility. It is hard to trust an approach that offers solutions that seem hypothetical, uncertain, and foreign to generations of experience. Trump offered to fix the problem in a way that was tangible, clear, respectful of their culture of work—and totally unrealistic.

However, no matter how much we try to understand the interests that drive people's attitudes, beliefs, and actions, we often run into a brick wall. Why do people so often seem to act *against* their own interests or believe patently false promises about dealing with the problems they face? So, while delving ever more deeply into Trump's supporters' interests and concerns is a necessary first step in understanding their beliefs and behavior, we must look beyond this. We have to move to the second question.

Identity, Community, and Purpose

Why do people act against what appears to be their self-interest? Why, for example, have many who benefit significantly from the Affordable Care Act supported Trump's efforts to dismantle it? Not because they are stupid but because there is something else at stake here. They are defending their sense of belonging, what gives meaning to their lives, and the community that has nurtured and defined them. Let's look at this more closely.

The power of Trump's rallies has been astonishing and frightening but also revealing. While all political rallies are meant to encourage a sense of our team versus their team, this is taken to a new height in Trump's rallies and is connected to an extreme level of disdain for those outside the Trump bandwagon. Trump has been a master at creating this bifurcation and using it to his advantage. Part of what his supporters seem to like is just how upset his opponents are with their fervid support of him. "Owning the libs" appears to be wonderfully motivating.

Underneath this, however, is a genuine sense that Trump represents and speaks to their sense of community and identity, and therefore they are going to support him no matter how outrageous or even unhinged he can get. The impeachment dramas only seem to have intensified this identification.

What has enabled this intense in-group and out-group dynamic, centered around the persona of Trump? The reasons for this are deeply interwoven with what has led to our extremely polarized political culture. Race has certainly played a role. Trump's barely concealed (or not concealed at all) racism has tapped into the feeling many of his supporters have that their place in the hierarchy of America's class system has been diminished by the empowerment and recognition of American's racial minorities, symbolized dramatically by the election of Barack Obama. But he is not the first to use race directly or implicitly. Nixon used it (that was a subtext of his embrace of the "Silent Majority"). Reagan raised the racially charged (and fallacious) specter of "welfare queens." George H.W. Bush used racial "dog whistles" in his 1988 presidential campaign (e.g. the Willie Horton ad). For the past 40 years, the Republican Party has sought to identify themselves with Southern Whites, particularly Evangelic Christians. Trump is the beneficiary and apotheosis of this long-term effort (Maxwell 2019).

But it's not just about race. Trump, as others before him, has appealed to a slew of identities and values that are increasingly clustered together. The politics of abortion, gun violence, affirmative action, LGBTQIA+ rights, drug policy, social safety nets, gender equality, healthcare, environmental protection, immigration, and the COVID-19 pandemic are all connected. Often these issues get attached to specific symbols, such as confederate statues, transgender use of public washrooms, teaching critical race theory, the protection of a particular species, or the wearing of face masks. It seems almost any issue can be escalated to the level of identity conflict—no matter how simple or straightforward it may seem.

These conflicts have become even more divisive due to the growing "stacking" of identities (Klein 2020). Where in the past there was a greater likelihood that we exhibited significant variation from one another in how our group identities came together, they have become far more likely to align in similar ways. Our religious affiliation, political orientation, geographical identity, and immigrant status are more likely to line up in consistent patterns. And this has tremendous ramifications for our approach to political issues. For example, a supporter of same-sex marriage is more likely to be pro-choice, pro-affirmative action, supportive of gun control, healthcare for all, and decisive climate policies. In the past, people's stance on one issue was less predictive of their stance on other issues than it is now, and this is a major source of our increasing polarization. Ezra Klein argues that this clustering phenomenon is far more important to people's political behavior than is their stance on particular issues:

> "Viscerally and emotionally, the stakes of politics we have evolved to sense is whether our group is winning or losing, whether the out-group is gaining the power to threaten us or whether our allies are amassing the strength to ensure our safety and prosperity. As our many identities merge into single political mega-identities, those visceral, emotional stakes are rising— and with them, our willingness to do anything to make sure our side wins."
> (Klein, *Why We're Polarized* [New York: Avid Reader Press, 2020], 75)

As important as this phenomenon may be, we have to remember that this is not a lockstep process. Just because someone supports the Black Lives Matter movement does not necessarily mean they are pro-choice or supporters of the Affordable Care Act. What Klein is arguing is that those associations are stronger than they used to be and therefore overlapping identities are less prevalent.

The Broken System

While identity considerations take us to a new level of depth in understanding conflict, they still place the issue inside us as individuals and communities. They also beg the questions of why we are seeing similar developments in very different societies. To get closer to the heart of these conflicts, we also have to look at their systemic roots.

The fervor that Trump evokes from his supporters is not an ahistorical or localized phenomenon. We have to consider why this is happening here, why now, and why are similar issues arising around the globe. To get at this, we need to understand the broadly held view that the systems we have built to govern our societies, educate us, keep us healthy, provide for our safety, and more generally intermediate between us and the world we live in have lost our confidence and trust. This deterioration in the public's confidence in our institutions includes but is most certainly not limited to Trump's supporters.

When we experience the unfairness and dysfunctionality of these systems, we can easily become overwhelmed by the seeming impossibility of understanding or navigating them. The systems that most closely affect our lives are often opaque, chaotic, and resistant to our efforts to influence them. So how do we respond?

We may rail against the "system," develop conspiracy theories, or look for scapegoats, such as minorities, immigrants, or other "others." We are often good at providing labels (e.g. the "swamp," the "deep state," "globalism," the "plutocracy," "corporate capitalism") that imply systems issues, but it is much more difficult to deconstruct just what is going on and how system change might be brought about. Instead, we are often drawn to disrupters, people who can force systems to change by taking decisive and sometimes outrageous actions to knock them out of their normal mode of operation.

Whether he understood this in systems terms or not, Trump played into this very directly and effectively when he promised to "drain the swamp" and dismantle the "deep state." He repeatedly said the system is broken and must be completely rebooted (or destroyed). Perhaps the most memorable line from his acceptance speech at the 2016 Republican convention was about this:

> "I have joined the political arena so that the powerful can no longer beat up on people that cannot defend themselves. Nobody knows the system better than me, which is why *I alone can fix it.*"
> (*Politico*, "Full text: Donald Trump 2016 RNC draft speech transcript," July 21, 2016)

Popular movements of a more progressive nature appeal to this same distrust and despair about the systems that govern our world. The energy behind the Black Lives Matter protests, while on the opposite end of the political and moral spectrum from the authoritarian populism of Trump, also arose out of centuries-long experiences with a system rigged against people of color, particularly African Americans. The call to defund the police is an essential recognition that the roots of police violence toward people of color lie in a racist system of policing and that unless this system is disrupted and even upended, individual incidents of racist behavior will continue unabated.

An important source of Bernie Sanders' appeal is his ability to attack the systemic roots of the major stresses people face in their lives. His discussion of systemic problems is much more detailed, strategic, consistent, and informed than Trump's. But, in one respect, the basic message is the same—unless the systems that govern so much of our lives are changed in fundamental ways, our problems won't go away.

At this level of understanding, we can discern the potential to break through some of our polarization and bring together people who in the end may be more antagonistic to a failed system than to each other. But we are very far from realizing that potential.

We can readily see the systemic roots of polarization and oppression if we look beyond individualistic explanations. But if we are to do something with that understanding, we have to delve into what we mean by systems, system dynamics, and system change.

System Concepts for Change

Throughout this book, we have discussed systems, disrupting systems, and system change. There are two reasons for this focus. One is that our most significant challenges are systemic in nature. Racism is an outgrowth of a system of White supremacy, which is itself an outgrowth of colonialism, which is an element of imperialism, which predates but is currently nested within globalism and capitalism. Climate change is systemic in nature and is in large part an outcome of globalism and capitalism as well, but exists at the intersection of human-created and natural systems. To maximize our capacity to encourage constructive conflict engagement and system change, we have to understand the systemic nature of the challenge. Secondly, system concepts, although often presented with a daunting amount of jargon and complexity, are extremely useful tools for both conflict interveners and social activists. So let's take a (relatively) simple approach to a complicated subject and delve into the conceptual world of systems.

What Do We Mean by Systems?

The vast literature on systems offers multiple approaches to understanding systems and to defining the term itself (see Gleick 2008; Pascale et al. 2000). Most definitions suggest two overarching meanings:

- Systems are collections of entities, units, or elements that are connected in some way.

- Systems are sets of principles or procedures that govern how players act—a methodology, so to speak.

A clock is a system. So is a family, the climate, the solar system, or the banking system. What connects the parts of systems can vary greatly: physical forces, biological ties, unspoken norms, laws, or formal structures governing membership and behavior. Two essential characteristics of systems are boundaries, which define— loosely or rigidly—who or what is part of the system, and the over- lapping structure of systems. All systems overlap or are part of other systems and contain subsystems of some kind.

This may seem like an obvious, almost trivial concept, but there are some interesting characteristics of systems, particularly com- plex systems, that can guide our understanding of social change and alert us to opportunities and barriers to change.

Types of Systems

Not only are there many types of systems, there are also numerous taxonomies of system types. Distinctions are often made, for exam- ple, between natural and manmade systems (e.g. the solar system and the family); cultural, economic, political, and interpersonal systems; closed and open systems; and static and dynamic systems.

For our purpose, a distinction between three types of systems seems useful.

Simple systems contain relatively few parts and given an encap- sulated set of information, their behavior is understandable and often predictable. For example, consider a cannon. If we know the force generated by the explosion of gunpowder, the angle at which the cannon is pointed, the force of gravity, the weight of the cannonball, the friction produced by air, and the contours of the immediate landscape, we can pretty much predict where the cannonball will land. Simple does not necessarily mean easy, as many first-year physics students may attest to.

Very little about human behavior, about systems of dominance and oppression, or about the challenge of sustainability can be understood as the operation of simple systems. Efforts to explain human interaction as simple systems are at best misleading and offer a false certainty about how the world works or how social problems can be solved. Families, for example, while often viewed as simple systems, are multigenerational, ever changing, and hard to define. We tend to view family problems as residing in individual members or at most a relationship between two people. Appraising the function of the family as a complex system is harder and figuring out how to intervene more confusing, but some of the most innovative approaches to family therapy have done just that (Bowen 1985; Haley 1987; Minuchin 1974).

Complicated systems contain many interacting elements and processes. For example, consider a cannon on a moving ship firing at another moving ship, both on a rolling sea. Or consider a weather forecast. In principle, if we had enough information, sophisticated enough algorithms, and unlimited computing resources, we should be able to predict whether there will be a thunderstorm at sea. And we certainly are a lot better at doing that than we used to be. But even with the most sophisticated computer modeling, the weather system is so interconnected with other complicated systems and the interactions among them so multi-faceted, that our success in forecasting the weather is partial and short term.

Our economic system is sometimes presented as a complicated system but one that can be understood and predicted with proper modeling. Economic modeling and forecasting are dependent on a set of assumptions about how rational actors will behave under different circumstances, and we are not always or perhaps ever completely rational beings. We are in fact nonlinear or complex adaptive systems and therefore so is the economy of which we are a part. The growing field of behavioral economics reflects this (Kahneman and Tversky 2013).

Complex adaptive systems (CASs) have the capacity to adapt, to change how they are structured or how they function in response to environmental input. For example, consider the path of a school of minnows in a pond. If a stick is plunged into the middle of this school as it is making its way around the pond, the school quickly reforms itself to move around the stick and continues on its way. The human brain is an immensely adaptive system. If one part of it is injured, the brain is often able to adapt to make up for the loss of functionality that may have resulted.

Virtually all organic systems are CASs as are all human-created systems (such as the economy). We can try to guide the functioning of these systems, but we can't determine how our interventions will work. Consider, for example, the educational system. Over many years, there have been efforts to address aspects of this system that have perpetuated racism and sexism. Generally these have had a more limited impact than hoped for because the elements of the system that perpetuated racist practices proved remarkably adaptable in their capacity to resist change. Laws, policies, and reforms are often less adaptive than the systems they were meant to change or maintain.

The implication of this for social change efforts is profound. To create change in a resilient and adaptive but oppressive system, we need to build resilient and adaptive movements. We need to act with an awareness of our limited capacity to predict how our efforts will play out or the impact they we will have, but we nonetheless need to act with determination and courage. As we shall see when we discuss sustainable disruption, the adaptable capacity of the systems we build to promote change are often more important for the prospects for change than are the specific tactics we employ at any given time.

How Systems Change

As recently as 2004, 60 percent of Americans opposed same-sex marriage. Fifteen years later, in 2019, 61 percent supported it (Pew Research Center 2019).

In 2004, the Defense of Marriage Act defining marriage as exclusive to heterosexual couples was the law of the land in the United States, and President George W. Bush was proposing a constitutional amendment to ban same-sex marriage. Today, marriage equality is a constitutional right. Canadian attitudes went through a similar transformation about ten years earlier (Keenan 2021). This is a phenomenal change in public attitudes and policy. Along with this has come a broad change in attitudes about gender and sexual orientation across almost all sectors of US and Canadian society. Of course, the struggle for equality and against discrimination of the LGBTQIA+ community continues, but the progress in this arena has been remarkable and is not matched by similar progress in attitudes toward racism, misogyny, disability, or ageism. We should take heart from the progress on marriage equality—and learn from it. What happened?

Five factors seem key: disruption, proximity, narratives, shared values, and the cost of change (Vedantam et al. 2019):

- *Disruption.* Starting at least as far back as the Stonewall riots of 1969, gay and lesbian activists engaged in confrontive acts to disrupt the system that forced them to remain hidden and fearful. The AIDS crisis saw many more acts of disruption against a power structure and medical system that was ignoring the tremendous pain and suffering in the gay community in particular.

- *Proximity.* LGBTQIA+ people exist in all communities, racial groups, classes, and ethnicities (even if it is not safe in all communities to be open about this). Therefore, as more and more people came out about their identity, people everywhere found they knew people and cared about people who had a different gender identity from what had previously been normative.

- *Narratives.* Stories of discrimination, suffering, and coming to terms with gender and sexuality made the abstract real and personal. They also made it clear that our gender and sexual identity are not choices we make but are an intrinsic part of who we are.

- *Shared values.* The marriage equality struggle in particular appealed to the commonalities that existed rather than the differences. Values of family, commitment, and love were at the center of this effort and appealed to universal human values.

- *Low cost.* As harsh and repressive as the oppression against the gay and lesbian communities has been, there was very little economic or social cost to granting marriage equality in particular and equal rights more generally. There were very few actual losers and lots of winners in the changing perceptions and policies about the LGBTQIA+ community.

Nonetheless, the change is still staggering. A deeply rooted set of cultural values and institutional discrimination seemed suddenly to disappear (although by no means completely). Systems of oppression can change, but the process requires engagement, disruption, a systemic approach, and luck.

Complex systems may be unpredictable, but that does not mean that intentional intervention is useless. On the contrary, grasping the limits of our capacity to predict and force change can simplify our task and concentrate our efforts. What is impossible for us as mediators, activists, therapists, or policymakers is to guarantee that our actions will lead to a particular kind of change. Instead, we can focus on how to precipitate a disruption of a system that will lead it to reorganize in some way, and we can try to guide that reorganization as best we can. We do this by making use of the emergent properties of a system—the capacity of a system to reorganize in the face of new inputs. How? The study of CASs suggests several approaches.

Nucleation. Nucleation occurs when specific changes force system reorganization. Requiring the use of body cameras by police officers, banning the use of nondisclosure agreements where harassment or bullying have occurred, placing carbon emission limits on the manufacture of new cars, or focusing on marriage equality in the effort to attain equal rights for the LGBTQIA+ communities can all be viewed as nucleation efforts. System disruption is seldom about attacking every element of a system at once. More often it requires selecting a target that is important, emotionally powerful, and connected at least symbolically to the system that is the ultimate target. Perhaps the most famous example of this in recent American history is Rosa Parks's (and other African Americans before her) refusal to sit in the back of a segregated bus.

Evan Wolfson, the primary instigator of the marriage equality movement, reflected on its success and impact on the fifth anniversary of the US Supreme Court Decision in *Obergefell v. Hodges* (its decision on marriage equality):

> "While neither the marriage nor employment win [a decision prohibiting discrimination in employment on the basis of sexual or gender identity] resolved every LGBTQ need, any more than the Civil Rights Act of 1964 cured all racism and sexism, the marriage conversation brought gay and trans people here and abroad new visibility, new allies, new power, and new acceptance for the cause of equality and in people's lives. The momentum from the marriage work continues to shape the public climate and helped lead to the Title VII victory. Wins are, indeed, the gifts that keep on giving."
> (Wolfson, "Five Years Later, How Obergefell Paved the Way for Bostock and the DACA Decision,"
> [*Slate*, June 20, 2020])

Feedback Loops. Systems change may occur as a result of feedback loops that promote or inhibit change. A feedback loop that is limited to the voices of those who benefit from the current functioning of a system will inhibit change. For example, social media and the proliferation of news sources often amplify the voices of those seeking to sustain an oppressive system. But they can also amplify calls for change, and no system can effectively suppress all feedback for change (although autocrats certainly try).

Freedom of information actions, whistleblower procedures, Ombuds offices, government inspector generals, and activist stockholders are all examples of efforts to change systems by changing the nature of the feedback loops that promote or inhibit system change. The effectiveness of public demonstrations is in part related to their ability to enter into the feedback processes of the systems they are calling out.

Bystanders with smartphones have significantly altered feedback loops concerning police community relations. The nine-minute video that Darnella Frazier took of George Floyd's murder, for example, undercut the official version initially promulgated by the Minneapolis Police Department. When it was posted online, it immediately went viral and led to massive protests throughout the United States and globally. The video proved crucial in the trial and conviction of Derek Chauvin. For this, Frazier received a Pulitzer Prize Special Citation. The Citation announcement made clear the importance of this in promoting social justice efforts:

> "For courageously recording the murder of George Floyd, a video that spurred protests against police brutality around the world, highlighting the crucial role of citizens in journalists' quest for truth and justice."
> (Pulitzer Prize Special Citations and Awards, "Special Citation to Darnella Frazier" [*Pulitzer Prizes*, 2021])

Energy Flow. CASs are not closed systems. They require the input of energy, the flow of energy through the system, and the discharge of energy from the system. The flow of energy into and out of systems is essential to their survival. Social change efforts inevitably involve attempts to introduce new sources of energy into systems or to disrupt the flow of energy through them so as to force systems to reorganize. An essential aspect of this is to disrupt the flow of power through systems.

One clear example of this is the role of social media. For better and for worse, social media has become a powerful force in mobilizing, organizing, and carrying out social actions. As activists use social media and related technology to plan actions, those in power may try to control social media, instigating efforts of others to find new platforms. China has gone to great extents to prevent communication among activists through banning rallies, closing news sources, arresting leaders, and tracking social media posts. At this point, this suppression appears to be working, but the last chapter has yet to be written, and activists in Hong Kong, while maintaining a lower public presence, have also been developing new means of communicating. As explained in a recent *Scientific American* article:

> "When you hit 'send' on a text message, it is easy to imagine that the note will travel directly from your phone to your friend's. In fact, it typically goes on a long journey through a cellular network or the Internet, both of which rely on centralized infrastructure that can be damaged by natural disasters or shut down by repressive governments. For fear of state surveillance or interference, tech-savvy protesters in Hong Kong avoided the Internet by using software such as FireChat and Bridgefy to send messages directly between nearby phones.
>
> "These apps let a missive hop silently from one phone to the next, eventually connecting the sender to the receiver—the only users capable of viewing the message. The collections of linked phones, known as mesh networks or mobile ad hoc networks, enable a flexible and decentralized mode of communication."
>
> (Houston-Edwards, "The Math of Making Connections" [*Scientific American*, April 2021], 22)

Conflict specialists also attempt to alter the flow of communications and power through a system of interaction by introducing new parties or altered processes to interactions. A three-way interaction, for example, produces considerably different dynamics than a one-on-one interchange. Much of what peace-building efforts are about involves introducing "third siders," creating new links among key actors, reinforcing "weak connections," all of which are about interfering with a destructive pattern of energy flow through systems and endeavoring to guide interactions in a more constructive way (Ury 2000; Coleman et al. 2008; Lederach 2005).

We are not suggesting that activists or peacemakers analyze or plan every action or intervention in accordance with the dynamics of CASs. However, system dynamics offer a useful way to understand our actions and choices, often as a means of spurring creativity and adaptability. They also provide a useful antidote to taking an overly linear approach to planning, one which assumes more predictability than is possible. Furthermore, if we really believe that racism, colonialism, homophobia, and misogyny are systemic problems, then part of our challenge is to grapple with the nature of these systems and how systems change might be promoted.

Are We Experiencing the Beginnings of a Paradigm Shift?

> ". . . when paradigms change, the world itself changes with them."
>
> (Kuhn, *The Structure of Scientific Revolutions* [Chicago: The University of Chicago Press, 1996], 111)

Systems can be resistant to change, but when change happens, it sometimes happens dramatically. Are we on the cusp of such a change in our foundational social systems? Are we at the crossroads of a paradigm shift? A paradigm is a theoretical framework which is universally recognized within a discipline (Kuhn 1996, x). As used in the social sciences, a paradigm is more than just a group of dominant principles; it reflects a particular worldview (i.e. how we understand reality) that is sustained as a normative force through our interactions (Stobbs 2011). A paradigm provides a common sense of reality, a shared worldview and values, and a common way to look at problems and solve them. If we do not share a paradigm, we can easily view each other as "crazy, stupid, and evil"; we are in a sense living in separate worlds. A paradigm dictates what we see, what we don't see, and what questions we ask. Paradigm shifts entail a completely new way of thinking, seeing, and doing. Could we be experiencing a shift in paradigm, without yet knowing what new paradigm will replace the old one or what new paradigm can guide us into the future?

The system disruption tactics discussed in this chapter are in a sense an effort to make room for new paradigms to emerge. But these approaches are grounded in an existing paradigm, which is based on White supremacy and imperialism. However, working within the existing paradigm may be the only way of shifting our ways of thinking and acting. Having policemen wear video cameras to provide evidence of the cruelty and oppressive tactics rampant within a White supremist system is a change mechanism solidly anchored in an existing system. But it is intended to change that system in some fundamental ways.

Borrowing from Kuhn (1996, 111), we may start seeing "new and different things when looking with familiar instruments in places [we] have looked before." Behavior that may have been normative may begin to be understood as an act that is nested in a web of relations that support and enable racism. The dramatic impact of the first pictures of Earth taken from space began to shift how we understood the nature of our existence. From experiences like this, we may start developing a new sense of reality—a shift in paradigm. The nature of paradigm shifts, however, is that they are extremely difficult to recognize in progress. They are often declared or predicted but less often actually experienced. And of course, new paradigms are not necessarily better ones.

A Return to Crazy, Stupid, and Evil: Are Racists Evil?

Let's reverse our journey for a moment. It's fine to delve into the nature of the systems that govern our lives, but what about our personal responsibility? For example, what about racists? Isn't racism in the end about people and not just systems? Don't we have to label racists as evil? Can't a focus on systems interfere with holding individuals accountable?

We have to distinguish between what motivates people to behave in a particular way and the behavior itself. We have no problem labeling racist behavior and speech (or violence against women, Asians, Muslims, or Jews) as immoral. Often it is critical to do so. But this is very different from working to develop a useful understanding of the fundamental source of this behavior and a plan for how to change the systems that permit, promote, and empower it. Of course, part of systems change is personal change. Holding ourselves to account for our behavior and our responsibility to confront behavior that is destructive can be part of how system change is brought about. But we always need to remember that racism resides in a system of institutions, policies, and norms that potentiate racist behavior and attitudes. By focusing solely on the morality or competence of the individual, we are avoiding an essential element of the challenge we face. We may feel better by labeling racists as evil, and in doing so we may contribute to a normative change in our tolerance for such behavior. But we are unlikely to either change the individual or disrupt the system if we do not connect the behavior to the system.

Our concepts about racial differences are rooted in the policies that promote those differences. To focus on individual or group attitudes or behavior independently of the system that fosters these contributes to the problem. According to Ibram Kendi:

> "We practice ethnic racism when we express a racist idea about an ethnic group or support a racist policy toward an ethnic group. Ethnic racism, like racism itself, points to group behavior, instead of policies, as the cause of disparities between groups."
>
> (Kendi, *How to Be an Antiracist* [New York: One World, 2019], 63)

The call to defund the police is about system change. If that remains the focus of the movement behind it, rather than solely on condemning the evil of the individual behavior of police officers, the chances for meaningful change will be enhanced. Of course, this does not mean that the behavior itself should be ignored. The stories of racist police behavior are essential to giving voice to the victims of police violence and to pointing out the systemic nature of the problem. The frequent chants of "I can't breathe" by protestors against police violence evoked the powerful image of George Floyd under the knee of Derek Chauvin. Was this emblematic of the behavior of a racist cop or the outgrowth of a racist system?

The tension between these two narratives is an old and essential one. Is the problem the behavior of a few "bad apple" police officers or the product of the very foundational philosophy and structure of policing itself? Chauvin's history and attitude make him a terrific candidate for those wishing to lay blame on evil individuals. But the history of police violence, the disproportionate number of African Americans, Brown people, and Latinx victims of this violence, and the origins of the modern concept of policing itself clearly point to the larger problem. The reactions to the "defund the police" slogan clearly illustrate this tension.

Crazy, stupid, and evil are labels we attach to individuals, but they are at root systemic concepts. They do not exist independently of the systems that define what is normative. When individuals change, they can be part of causing systems to change. When we understand crazy, stupid, and evil as products of a system, rather than something that resides in individuals, we are contributing to both systems change and individual growth.

Reflective Dialogue: Our Use of Attributions

Bernie: A confession. I use stupid, crazy, and evil attributions all the time. Trump was probably a bit of all three. During the height of the pandemic, when I was confronted with someone who refused to get vaccinated or wear masks in indoor settings, it was hard for me to avoid personality-based attributions. And I don't think we always should. Our anger and frustration are guides as well as our more reasoned processes are. People acting in ways that seem wrong, dangerous, and irrational are part of the picture. Sometimes they need to be called out. My concern as we have discussed throughout this chapter is that relying on this as an explanation obscures the deeper and longer-term roots of oppression, war, and environmental degradation. You and I have frequently exchanged such attributions about institutions and individuals we have encountered. Were we wrong to do so?

Jackie: We certainly have used these attributions. I believe that someone like Derek Chauvin is evil in the sense that his actions are highly immoral and wicked. I also believe that naming these behaviors in the ways that we see them and experience them is important if we want to make systemic change. Staying neutral or being dishonest about how we feel will not lead to change. Of course, this means that there will be others who think we are evil, crazy, or stupid and will label us as such. What we cannot do is leave it at that. We must dig deeper into the roots of behavior. What systems have allowed or even encouraged racist behavior? If we want systemic change, we must be willing to have difficult conversations with those who do not think or see events in the same way we do. I also try to never lose hope that most people, even those I have labeled as evil, have the capacity to change. Some days it is harder than others to hang on to this hope.

part three

strategic disruption

chapter seven

from chaotic to strategic disruption

"Do not get lost in a sea of despair. Be hopeful, be optimistic. Our struggle is not the struggle of a day, a week, a month, or a year, it is the struggle of a lifetime. Never, ever be afraid to make some noise and get in good trouble, necessary trouble."

—John Lewis

"In order for us as poor and oppressed people to become part of a society that is meaningful, the system under which we now exist has to be radically changed … It means facing a system that does not lend itself to your needs and devising means by which you change that system."

—Ella Baker

Building and sustaining social movements requires cooperation, competition, dialogue, escalation, coalition building, developing short-term goals, and keeping an eye on the long road to change. Planning is important, but so is adaptability and flexibility. And all of this requires a never-ending effort to deepen our understanding of the nature of the forces resisting and promoting change.

Each of these elements of change is critical to establishing effective social movements. But they are not enough. Among the most significant barriers activists face are the powerful but incomplete narratives about how change occurs. In the news media, popular culture, and most history classes we are offered stories of change that can distort our focus and guide us away from the critical role of social movements. We are told, for example, that:

- Change occurs through legal and legislative efforts. Whom we elect is the key element. Our focus should be on electoral politics.

- Dialogue, negotiation, and relationship building are the essential ingredients to change. Our efforts should be centered on whom we reach out to and how we find win-win outcomes.

- Change is both impossible and inevitable. Fundamental change is impossible, but if we work within the system, change will happen.

- Heroic or at least effective leaders are the essential drivers of change.

Of course, these narratives are so powerful because there is an element of truth in each of them. Electing progressive leaders is important. So is dialogue. We are truly engaged in struggles against deeply entrenched systems, but change does occur. Leaders make a difference.

But these messages are dangerously incomplete and have the cumulative effect of guiding our attention away from the need to disrupt systems, to build movements, and to get into "good trouble." Without social movements, especially ones skilled at navigating these seemingly contradictory demands (engage, escalate; think long term, seize the moment; organize to vote, organize for change), social change will be shallow, ephemeral, or nonexistent.

This chapter focuses on the more uncomfortable and often polarizing aspects of change—chaos, disruption, escalation, and confrontation. To be sure, bringing people together, dialogue, and constructive engagement are important, but the less "nice" side of the process is also essential, and one way power structures maintain themselves is by avoiding, denigrating, and punishing these elements.

As discussed in Chapter 2, an exclusive focus on dialogue and negotiation is a trap that conflict practitioners are particularly prone to. John Lande, a mediator and professor emeritus of Dispute Resolution at the University of Missouri School of Law, had this to say about the role of dispute resolution professionals in social change:

> "I think that fundamental progress generally comes from sustained nonviolent social and political action over extended periods that substantially changes public opinion. That is what forces entrenched interests to surrender some political power.
>
> Given this, I don't expect that our field will be a major player in such social change efforts. It would be nice if we could mediate major social conflicts to produce equitable positive-sum outcomes that most people feel good about. Unfortunately, I think that the world doesn't work that way in polarized eras (if ever).
>
> In these times, I think it's important to strategically promote or provide advocacy involving constructive conflict engagement rather than neutral conflict resolution. We can help identify parties and stakeholders that will act (or can be induced to act) in good faith, and we can limit our work to engage only with such people."
>
> (Lande, "ADR's Place in Navigating a Polarized Era"
> [indisputably.org, 2021])

Whether the field of ADR (alternative dispute resolution) has a major role to play in social change efforts is not in our opinion a productive question. Professions are generally too much part of the system they are trying to change to be a significant source of disruption to that system. However, the experience, knowledge, training, and skills that each of us brings can contribute to change efforts. And those of us who work on conflict have considerable experience with what causes it, what makes it effective, and how disruption can work. We just have to remember that we are part of a system that is more interested in maintaining itself than in changing. This includes those who provide funding for social movements but who have derived their wealth from the system that these movements are trying to change (Giridharadas 2018). With that understanding, we all have a role to play in working to change systems that perpetuate oppression and endanger our world.

Good Trouble

Social movements do not disrupt entrenched systems by being nice. They do so by escalation, by forcing reactions from those in power, by building support across increasing swaths of society, and by interfering in some way with the normal operations of systems. This does not require being meanspirited or dismissive of those they disagree with, but disruption often involves a genuine and not always well-regulated or controlled display of anger and disapproval. The boundaries between responses that are strong, determined, and emotionally authentic and those that are hostile and insulting are porous and easily breached. The art of building sustainable and effective social movements involves an ongoing effort to honor these boundaries, to treat those in opposition to change as human beings whose beliefs and actions must be challenged but who are also capable of change and of eventually becoming allies. Easier said than done, especially since the path to sustainable and strategic system disruption usually involves a period of chaos.

The Power and Limits of Chaos

"Effective efforts at disruption have the potential to push systems toward the 'edge of chaos'—that sweet spot where a system faces enough disorganization and upheaval so that it is compelled to adapt to the forces pushing for change but not so much that it ceases to be able to function or even to exist" (Pascale, Millemann, and Gioja 2000, 61). Of course, some systems are so fundamentally problematic that they should indeed cease to function, but even the most revolutionary change efforts build on existing systems. Even Vladimir Lenin, the leader of the 1917 Russian Revolution (and not one to oppose chaos, violence, or authoritarianism) said:

> "We are not utopians, we do not 'dream' of dispensing at once with all administration, with all subordination. ... No, we want the socialist revolution with people as they are now, with people who cannot dispense with subordination, control, and 'foremen and accountants.'"
>
> (Lenin, *The State and Revolution* [1917], Chapter 3)

Not all disruption, even strategic disruption, is planned. Sometimes externalities such as climate change or economic crises act to create disruption. For example, the dramatic increase in virtual interactions, distance learning, and dispersed workplaces brought about by COVID-19 have had a dramatic impact on virtually all of the systems we are part of—and many of these changes will prove to be irreversible. Often strategic and intentional efforts at disruption are instigated by externalities of this nature or by precipitating events that were not part of a planned change effort. In fact, the success of social movements depends on circumstances beyond anyone's control lining up in a way that reinforces change efforts. In other words, luck plays an important role.

The intentional efforts of social movements are nonetheless essential to fundamental change. Although movements may appear to arise overnight in response to particular events (e.g. the Arab Spring in response to the self-immolation of a street vendor in Tunis in protest of arbitrary action taken by police against his fruit stand, or the rise of the civil rights movement in response to Rosa Parks's historic ride at the front of a Montgomery bus), their roots are almost always deeper and more intentional than they might have initially appeared to be. Rosa Parks, for example, was an experienced activist and was selected for this role by the National Association for the Advancement of Colored People (NAACP) after previous efforts did not generate the hoped-for response.

A Balance between the Strategic and the Chaotic

For the disruptions that social movements bring to be effective, they have to endure in the face of the inevitable pushback of the systems seeking to resist change and the ups and downs that change efforts always face. But more than simply enduring, these movements have to grow, become more structured, and develop systems of interaction, leadership, decision making, and alliance building. In other words, the disruption has to become more strategic over time and the movements more organized. Such has been the case with almost all fundamental change efforts.

But if movements are too planned, they also can lose the dynamism and ability to react quickly and creatively to changing circumstances that make them effective. Over time, effective efforts at system disruption will become less chaotic and more strategic, but an element of the chaotic, unpredictable, and uncontrollable will always be present. For example, peaceful protests are often overshadowed by very minor acts of violence or looting. The highly disciplined nonviolent strategies of the organized civil rights movement were punctuated by riots. Often, authorities have tried, sometimes effectively, to provoke such a response in order to discredit a movement. We certainly saw that attempted during the summer of 2020 in response to the Black Lives Matter protests.

However, it is important to remember that chaotic disruption is not the same as violence (nor is strategic disruption equivalent to nonviolence). It is tempting to simply dismiss this chaos as an unfortunate side effect of an intense confrontation and not genuinely part of the movement for change, but broad efforts at system disruption are themselves complex adaptive systems, and the chaotic aspects—if they do not overwhelm the strategic elements—are a necessary part of them.

An important source of the power of nonviolent strategy lies in its capacity to disrupt systems, taking them to the brink of, but not over the edge into chaotic and even violent dissolution. But approaching this edge is not easy or comfortable and is likely to provoke resistance not only from the power structure but from more established movement groups.

The Rocky Flats Nuclear Weapons Plant Story

In the stormy early morning hours of April 29, 1978, the three of us were suddenly awoken by a group of heavily armed men in camouflage. I (Bernie) was sleeping in the back of a station wagon along with two others, outside the Rocky Flats Nuclear Weapons Plant, 8 miles south of Boulder, Colorado. The day before, about 7,000 people had gathered near the gates of the weapons facility to protest the production of nuclear weapons as a "local hazard, global threat." The original plan was for the rally to be followed by a sit-in of about 300 people on the railroad track that led to the plant and was the route by which supplies were taken in and nuclear triggers (plutonium bombs) shipped out. Participants and organizers expected arrests to occur within a day or two, ending the protest and setting the stage for court hearings that could be the focus of further actions.

(Continued)

(*Continued*)

I was one of the organizers of the protest (as were the other two) and had conducted a series of trainings in nonviolence for people who would serve as peacekeepers and for those who were planning to take part in civil disobedience. The three of us were not planning to join the sit-in ourselves, but that night it seemed as if that was exactly what we were doing. We were concerned about those camping out on the tracks because of the cold, rainy weather, so we brought food, hot drinks, blankets, ponchos, and the like to those sitting in. We insisted that some who were showing signs of hypothermia leave to dry off and warm up. We camped out in the car.

The rally had been organized under the auspices of several peace groups, including the Mobilization for Survival, Fellowship of Reconciliation, and the American Friends Service Committee. They had carefully planned the action and coordinated with local law enforcement and the security service at the plant. They had not planned on the arrival of a heavily armed SWAT team in the middle of the night. Nor had they planned on the determination of those sitting in to continue to do so after the initial arrests were made.

As soon as we saw the armed men, the three of us roused ourselves, jumped out of the car, and intercepted the SWAT team, who insisted they just wanted to check on how everyone was doing. We believed they were trying to intimidate all of us but decided to take them at their word for the moment. We did our best to slow everything down, asking for some time to alert the demonstrators to what was happening, to select a couple of spokespersons, and to monitor the interchange. It all went smoothly enough under the circumstances (and we later asked the plant to make sure that this type of surprise did not happen again—it didn't). The

SWAT team's arrival actually energized the protesters and convinced them that what they were doing was important.

What did not go so well was the communication between the original organizers and those who wanted to continue the sit-in. This was not going according to the carefully developed plans of the more established groups who felt that their efforts were being discounted and their plans undermined. Those who had committed themselves to the sit-in felt that symbolic actions were not enough. They were determined to do all they could to disrupt the production of nuclear weapons. There were some tense interchanges, but in the end, it became clear to all that the protests had taken on a life of their own and that the original organizers would have to accept this and, if possible, embrace it.

Thus was born the Rocky Flats Truth Force, which organized the ongoing occupation of the track for over a year and which spawned many subsequent actions. The Rocky Flats Nuclear Weapons Plant was closed in 1992. Truth Force Members were instrumental in starting the Rocky Mountain Peace and Justice Center, which continues to promote anti-war and anti-racism actions to this day. They were important participants in the negotiations about how the site should be cleaned up and what should happen to it after it was decommissioned. One of them later became mayor of Boulder.

The dynamic that played out at Rocky Flats between the more established movement groups and those spontaneously arising as actions took place is not unusual. There is often tension between the more disciplined approach represented by better funded and organized groups and the more decentralized and fluid approach of groups like the Truth Force. We have seen this, for example, in the civil rights movement (SNCC, the Black Panthers, and now the Black Lives Matter activists vs. the Southern Christian Leadership Conference and the NAACP), the environmental movement (the Sierra Club, Audubon Society, and National Resource Defense Council vs. Earth First, Greenpeace, and Extinction Rebellion).

Each of these organizations brings something needed, and each brings liabilities as well. Spontaneous or emergent elements bring dynamism, excitement, necessary chaos, and "good trouble, necessary trouble." But they are prone to either fading away or gradually becoming more established themselves and are less effective at the ongoing and often tedious work of day-to-day organizing. More established groups are better able to marshal resources and develop deeper links to communities, local institutions such as churches and citizen advocacy groups, and elected leaders. But they are often threatened by the unpredictability and chaos that spontaneously arising groups are likely to represent and that excite broader participation and are essential to challenging the structures of reaction and oppression.

Strategic and Chaotic Disruption

The line between chaotic, unplanned, and spontaneous disruption and carefully planned and coordinated strategic disruption is a thin one and at times nonexistent. The instigators of the sit-ins at Rocky Flats, for example, had a clear strategic sense that there needed to be a long-term plan to keep the pressure on and to keep the issue in the public eye. They also understood their efforts to be part of an ongoing struggle against nuclear armaments. But the immediate decision to stay on the tracks and to return again and again after being arrested and released arose out of the opportunity presented by a specific moment in time.

A strategic approach to disruption does not require that everything be planned out or carefully orchestrated. As we discussed in the previous chapter, when dealing with complex systems, adaptability is at least as important as planning, and the essence of planning may be preparing to be adaptable. What separates chaotic disruption from strategic disruption and what is essential to its power is its unpredictability and uncontrollability.

Long-term engagement in social change requires a strategic vision of how to build a movement that can challenge power structures over time. Strategic disruption is a constantly evolving process that has several key characteristics:

- *Awareness:* A recognition that the current system is exploitative. This includes self-awareness as to our role—intentional or not—in supporting such systems. In developing our awareness, we start moving away from blaming individuals and toward focusing on the systemic roots of oppression.

- *Relationship-building:* The critical component in complex systems is not individual performance but rather the way individuals interact within and across systems. Fostering a culture that nurtures relationships with allies and is open to forming connections across differences is characteristic of strong and sustainable social movements.

- *Participation:* Related to a focus on relationship, creating a movement that encourages broad participation across many social elements is also essential to success (Chenoweth and Stephan 2011). This relates to both individual participation and organizational support. The Arab Spring uprising ended in disappointment across many societies, but Tunisia seems to have been an exception. Tunisia emerged from the Arab Spring with a democratic constitution (although a fragile one). An important factor was the role played by their largest union, business organizations, lawyer associations, and human rights groups, who came together to establish a "national dialogue quartet" that led talks among rival factions culminating in democratic elections and a new constitution (Taub 2016). The work of the quartet was recognized with the Nobel Peace Prize in 2015.

- *Improvisation and adaptation:* As previously discussed, complex systems cannot be completely controlled, so movements need to be willing to expect the unexpected, to be flexible, and to develop their capacity to improvise. How decision making is structured, how leadership is exercised, and how risk taking is guided are critical contributors or deterrents to adaptability.

- *Reflection and learning:* The flipside of adaptability is reflection and learning. Effective movements require self-reflection and constructive self-criticism. Developing a culture conducive to constructive and frank reflection is important to nurture the capacity to adapt to changing circumstances.

- *Vision:* In the end, what makes disruption strategic and not chaotic is a vision of the goals and values of a movement and the means of furthering these. Developing such a vision is a continuous effort and the vision needs to be both flexible and consistent. But without this, confusion and divisiveness are likely to undercut sustainability.

- *Attention to power dynamics:* Where efforts at constructive engagement often fall short is their failure to adequately attend to the role of power. White supremacy is essentially about the elite maintaining and exerting power over others. The fundamental obstacle to dealing with climate change is the benefit that powerful segments of society gain from current policies and the way in which these benefits have become baked into our social structure. Social movements are about exposing, understanding, and challenging these power relationships. To do so, they must remain attuned to the power, racial, and gender dynamics within the movement itself.

- *Preparing for the long term:* System change does not come easily or quickly. Strategic disruption efforts may happen in waves, but we need to understand the long-term challenges and to prepare as best we can for these. We need to anticipate the likelihood of setbacks, to build on successes, and to develop sustainable structures for change.

As might be readily apparent, these themes are covered in one form or another throughout this book. How they come together is critical to social change efforts.

The Power of Nonviolence (and the Choices It Offers)

Does unpredictability go hand in hand with violence? Chaotic disruption does not mean violent disruption nor does strategic disruption necessarily rule that out. Random acts of violence are often byproducts of the anger and energy that also lead to chaotic disruption—but they are not the same thing. Some social change organizations that have embraced sabotage have done so in a strategic (if not necessarily effective) way. Earth First, the Weathermen, and Umkhonto (an offshoot of the African National Congress—discussed in Chapter 1) are examples of movement groups that saw the use of sabotage as a legitimate strategy to promote social change. Who defines what is violent and under what circumstances it is legitimate is itself a product of a White supremacist society. Our concern with violence as a strategy is that it is neither effective nor sustainable, but violence is not what defines disruptive acts as chaotic and nonviolence does not make them strategic.

Guns in Mississippi

Gunfire rang out in the middle of the night—an attack by the KKK of Kosciusko, Mississippi, on the Freedom House, which was operated under the auspices of the Mississippi Freedom Democratic Party. Two people were wounded (not severely). It was January 1966. I (Bernie) had traveled along with about 20 mostly White students from Oberlin College to conduct an intensive voter registration effort. Six of us were staying in the Freedom House. Along with most of us, I was asleep when this happened. But I jumped up, grabbed a shotgun, and headed to the front door. Two or three others who were awake succeeded in getting shots off in the direction of the fleeing car, but by the time I got to the door, the car was gone. The incident made headlines in papers around the country and was covered on national television. I am on record (on the *Today* show no less) as supporting the use of guns in defense of our place of residence. What on earth were we doing, participating in a movement committed to nonviolence, armed and, more importantly, ready to use our weapons if necessary?

Gunter Frentz, the staff organizer assigned to Kosciusko by the Mississippi Freedom Democratic Party, had been a close friend of Mickey Schwerner, a civil rights activist who, along with James Chaney and Andrew Goodman, was murdered by the KKK and their supporters the previous summer. Gunter felt we needed to be armed to protect ourselves, and we went along with his advice. To my knowledge, there were no further violent efforts to disrupt voter registration efforts in Attala County, where Kosciusko is located. So in one sense our response to the attack on us worked. More importantly, this was a significant disruptive event. The White power structure was not prepared for an armed response and the national attention it brought. Perhaps this was an effective effort to promote system change.

Maybe, but I have come to feel there were some major problems with what we did and that this could easily have blown up in a very dangerous way. We may have actually interfered with the development of a sustainable change effort in Attala County and beyond. We were mostly White, mostly young (I was 19), from a very different social milieu, and were in Kosciusko for only about 10 days. The most likely repercussions were going to occur after we had been long gone, and while many of us remained activists for the long haul, only one of us returned to this community. Was it up to us to take this step? Were we even aware of the havoc we could have brought down on the local Black community? As it turned out, they were very supportive of us. Many were armed themselves, and the guns we had were mostly supplied by Black families.

What is striking to me on a personal level is how readily I crossed a line without fulling considering the consequences. As a group, we never fully discussed the implications of being armed or of how we would respond if in fact we were attacked. And when we were, we instinctively chose to cross the line from a nonviolent to a violent response. I never got a shot off, but I was certainly intending to do that if possible. What we did brought some immediate positive results, but what about the long-term implication? This was one of many events that began to undercut the strict adherence to nonviolence that had previously characterized the civil rights movement. To this day, I am ambivalent about the wisdom of our actions. This was definitely a system disrupter, but a strategic one, at least for me, it was not. (For a fuller description of this incident and its implications and aftermath, see Rinaldi 2021.)

Whether one embraces nonviolence from a Gandhian pacifist ethic or from a strategic and situational analysis, two elements are always critical: taking the moral high ground and acting to challenge an oppressive system in a way that demands a response. When acts of violence occur, those in power will draw as much attention to these as they possibly can and away from the underlying oppression that led to them. Furthermore, those in control of the state apparatus or dominant structure are better equipped to engage in violence than those seeking change. But they are in a relatively less powerful position to counter the expression of massive numbers of protesters who are not attempting to contend with the power structure on the basis of armed might but on the field of values and the will of the people.

Nonviolent disruption is based on the belief that ultimately, even in dictatorships, the leaders of government are dependent on the consent of the governed (Sharp 1973). In a study of historical violent and nonviolent civil uprisings, Chenoweth and Stephan found that nonviolent uprisings were much more likely to result in regime change than were violent ones. They concluded:

> ". . . nonviolent campaigns have a participation advantage over violent insurgencies, which is an important factor in determining campaign outcomes. The moral, physical, informational, and commitment barriers to participation are much lower for nonviolent resistance than for violent insurgency. Higher levels of participation contribute to a number of mechanisms necessary for success, including enhanced resilience, higher probabilities of tactical innovation, expanded civic disruption (thereby raising the costs to the regime of maintaining the status quo), and loyalty shifts involving the opponent's erstwhile supporters, including members of the security forces. Mobilization among local supporters is a more reliable source of support than the support

of external allies which violent campaigns must obtain to compensate for their lack of participants."
    (Chenoweth and Stephan, *Why Civil Resistance Works: The Strategic Logic of Nonviolent Conflict* [New York: Columbia University Press, 2011], 23–24)

Chenoweth and Stephan emphasize the key role of participation and argue that violence or the threat of it drives down participation and inhibits the capacity of social movements to endure against the inevitable pushback of those in power. This was one of Bernie's concerns about taking up arms in Mississippi. Today, voting rights are under assault across the United States. A movement to resist this is developing, and its success will be critical to the future of American democracy. Part of this movement will involve voter registrations and mobilization. But more than this will be necessary. The hard work done to achieve access to the ballot box over the past 70 years needs to continue.

How exactly can a system be disrupted by nonviolent action? Strikes, boycotts, mass demonstrations, art, sit-ins, legal action, and guerilla theater are among many nonviolent approaches we can imagine. Sharp (1973) identifies 198 different tactics that have been effectively employed at various times during the past century. The effectiveness of any given action or movement depends on its disruptive power, the popular support it generates, the capacity of the power structure to suppress a movement, and luck. Of course, not all efforts succeed, and the price activists pay, no matter how successful the effort, can be enormous.

Enduring Disruption

In 2019–2020, massive protests occurred in Hong Kong, a former British colony that was transferred back to China in 1997. Hong Kong's current political structure, referred to as "one country, two systems," has a separate legal and judiciary system from China and more freedom of assembly and speech. When new legislation was proposed that would allow extradition of criminal suspects from Hong Kong to China, Hongkongers organized massive demonstrations in opposition for fear of China using the extradition law as a tool of repression. The proposed law was eventually withdrawn. But then China struck back with a vengeance, arresting protest leaders and promulgating new "national security" laws with harsh penalties for dissidents. As with many of the Arab Spring countries, what seemed to be a promising movement for change was at least for now suppressed.

These are discouraging setbacks, but not surprising ones. As discussed in Chapter 5, we are dealing with enduring issues, and the process of change does not occur in a neatly scripted three-act play. At this writing, massive street demonstrations are occurring in Tunisia to protest the president's power grab and creative and ongoing resistance continues in Hong Kong. Multiple levels of organizing are occurring in the United States to protect and restore voting rights. In the face of an alarming series of droughts, fires, hots spells, floods, and cold spells that signal the rapid advance of climate change, action also is escalating on many fronts to insist that decisive steps be taken to combat global warming. We can't know where this will all take us because we are dealing with complex and unpredictable dynamics. What is clear is that ongoing disruption of existing systems will have to be part of the picture if we are to help bend the arc of history toward justice.

What will promote the sustainable disruption necessary to obtain profound change? Once again, the central requirements for this are clarity of vision, a systems perspective, and the development of communities of change. As activists, we need to concentrate on the immediate and local for tactical purposes while we keep our focus on the global and long term to guide our overall approach. This means building strong and diverse means of communicating with each other and with the communities we are part of. It means framing everything we do in terms of both the immediate target and long-term goals. And it means building organizational structures to endure in the face of repression and pushback.

The most powerful movements are decentralized, democratic, adaptable, and inclusive. Histories of social movements often focus on (mostly male) heroic leaders, but the broader the base of decision making, the more non-hierarchical the structure, the more likely a movement can endure. Leaders can be attacked, removed, or murdered. They can prove to be ineffective, authoritative, or exploitative. Centralized organizations can be infiltrated, attacked, deflected, and isolated. Leaders are important, as discussed in the next chapter, but to the extent everyone is a leader and a follower, a movement is more likely to endure. Inclusivity means diversity and attention to racial and gender dynamics. Racist power structures have always used racism itself to undercut change efforts. These efforts can and must be resisted.

Now, folks, you've come to the hardest time.
The boss will try to bust your picket line.
He'll call out the police, the National Guard,
They'll tell you it's a crime to have a union card.
They'll raid your meetin', they'll hit you on the head,
They'll call every one of you a goddam red,
Unpatriotic, communist spies, sabotaging national defense!
But out at Ford, here's what they found,
And out at Vultee, here's what they found,
And out at Allis-Chalmers, here's what they found,
And down at Bethlehem, here's what they found:
That if you don't let red-baiting break you up,
And if you don't let stoolpigeons break you up,
And if you don't let vigilantes break you up,
And if you don't let race hatred break you up,
You'll win.
What I mean, take it easy, but take it!

(The Almanac Singers. "Talking Union." Track 3 on *The Original Talking Union & Other Union Songs*. Folkway Records [now part of Smithsonian Folkways], 1955.)

Storytelling and Social Media

When Gene Sharp created his list of 198 acts of nonviolent action, when Ella Baker and John Lewis were organizing civil rights protests, or when Pete Seeger and Woody Guthrie were recording the *Talking Union*, there was no Internet, Facebook, or Twitter. Today, social movements sometimes seem to occur almost entirely online, although as Alicia Garza has argued, that is a myth (Garza 2020). But what all these efforts, past and present, have in common is storytelling. We gather together, empower each other, build a common purpose, and convey our message through the stories we tell. The #MeToo and Black Lives Matter movements began and grew through storytelling. The songs that Pete Seeger, Woody Guthrie, and others sang to workers trying to organize in the 1930s and the examples of our participation in conflict engagement and social movement spread through this book are stories to help us grow, to solidify our purpose, and to translate between theory and practice.

Social media has enabled some of our most poignant individual stories to go viral (a term that would have made no sense 20 years ago) and have both connected us and divided us. It's hard to imagine a contemporaneous social change effort that does not involve a significant social media presence. So we end this chapter with each of us telling of a story that we were exposed to through social media and that has influenced our own involvement and commitment to social change.

Reflective Dialogue: Inspirational Stories That Went Viral
Bernie: Before she started her solo Skolstrejk för klimatet (School Strike for Climate) in Sweden, Greta Thunberg was unknown to the world. That was in August 2018, when she was 15 years old. In December 2019, just 16 months later, she appeared on the cover of *Time* magazine when she was

named its person of the year. *Time* described the impact she has had:

> "[Thunberg] has succeeded in creating a global attitudinal shift, transforming millions of vague, middle-of-the-night anxieties into a worldwide movement calling for urgent change. She has offered a moral clarion call to those who are willing to act, and hurled shame on those who are not. She has persuaded leaders, from mayors to Presidents, to make commitments where they had previously fumbled: after she spoke to Parliament and demonstrated with the British environmental group Extinction Rebellion, the U.K. passed a law requiring that the country eliminate its carbon footprint. She has focused the world's attention on environmental injustices that young, indigenous activists have been protesting for years. Because of her, hundreds of thousands of teenage "Gretas," from Lebanon to Liberia, have skipped school to lead their peers in climate strikes around the world" (Alter et al. 2019).

Thunberg has addressed the UN Conference on Climate Change, the Davos Forum, testified to Congress, the UK Parliament, been nominated three times (and counting) for the Nobel Peace Prize, has gone head-to-head with President Trump (on Twitter) and came out on top, and the list goes on. She is not an organizer, insists she is not a leader, but she has established a powerful voice, one that is clear, unambiguous, and above all, truthful. The "Greta Phenomenon" largely came to be through social media. When Thunberg

(*Continued*)

(*Continued*)

started her strike, she sat alone, but she posted a picture of herself with her sign on Instagram and Twitter. This was quickly reposted by youth activists elsewhere and then by environmental activists globally. She now has millions of followers on social media, and her tweets are reposted to millions more. Thunberg is a disrupter in the best sense of the word.

Her impact on me is a constructive paradox. By calling out the danger of climate change in unambiguous and stark terms, she has placed a magnifying glass on just how scary our world is, but she has done so in a way that has demanded action rather than despair. As a result, I have become more hopeful about the future.

Jackie: Tarana Burke is a Black activist woman who in 2007 created a movement to give a voice to women who had been victims of sexual harassment and assault (García 2017). The movement was mostly unknown until actress Alyssa Milano tweeted #MeToo when sexual assault accusations were brought against Harvey Weinstein. The #MeToo movement became a worldwide phenomenon and, in the process, provided a powerful new voice for sexually abused women everywhere (García 2017). In an interview with Colleen Walsh (2020) for the *Harvard Gazette*, Burke said:

> "What I think, and I hope, is that we're in a place that's moving away from the individual headlines and salacious stories about accusations being made toward individuals, and thinking more collectively about what we can do to end sexual violence and how we are shifting the focus away from individual bad acts and moving it toward the systemic cause of sexual violence."

Burke knows the power of turning an individual story into a collective story. She is keenly aware that by sharing our collective stories, we can simultaneously heal and dismantle oppressive structures. We can construct together a forward-looking story. Through the collective stories of sexual abuse, the individual suffering and agency of the abused are acknowledged. The #MeToo movement revealed the intricate web of systemic sexual abuse. It is a reminder of the power of stories to challenge a system that allows sexual abuse to proliferate.

chapter eight

allies, teams, and leaders

Social change is a social process. To change systems, we need to build systems for change. That means reaching out to potential allies, becoming allies ourselves, developing leadership structures that reflect the strategic aims and values we are pursuing, and connecting across our differences. We subscribe to the principle of treating everyone as potential allies and leaders (but also holding everyone—ourselves included—accountable for our actions).

Activists frequently experience the tension between wanting to build an expansive movement characterized by broad allegiances, open membership, and efforts to engage with those we disagree with and needing to build focused, well-organized, strategic, committed structures that can endure the inevitable stresses of social action. This tension is long-standing, and how it is navigated defines the nature of the effort.

At times, it feels impossible to talk with others who think differently than we do. The divisions in our world seem to be getting worse. People are hesitant about engaging in authentic conversations because they fear they may unintentionally hurt someone's feelings, damage a relationship, trigger conflict, or be subject to reprisals.

But if we want to be catalysts for systemic change, building relationships with natural allies as well as with those with whom we have important disagreements is essential. How do we nurture alliances in a highly polarized environment? What role do leaders play in creating the spaces for productive relationships to flourish?

In this chapter, we draw on our experiences in helping people bridge their differences, work together in more effective ways, and deal with conflicts in a principled way to consider how to build and sustain the alliances essential to social change efforts.

Team Leadership and Leadership of Teams

Adaptive systems require adaptive leadership structures, and top-down leadership is seldom especially adaptive. To organize social change within communities or institutions requires developing leadership throughout the systems in which we operate. Borrowing on the checkered experience of Coalition Forces in Iraq, we need a "team of teams" approach to leadership (McChrystal et al. 2015). In a team of teams, relationships among the different parts of a system are everyone's responsibility. In Iraq, that meant arranging for "everyone to know *someone* on every team, so that when someone in a team had to reach out or collaborate with someone outside their team, they could see or envision a friendly face" (ibid, 129). This is a means to break down the silos and build relationship networks that can adapt to rapidly evolving circumstances. The goal is to have everyone *see* where they fit in the system and understand they are in an interdependent relationship with each other—part of a larger system—"not cogs in a system" (ibid, 175).

According to General (ret.) Stanley McChrystal, a successful team of teams requires the following (McChrystal 2015):

- Shared consciousness, which is achieved when all the teams think and act as one. To achieve shared consciousness, every member of every team needs to have a "holistic understanding" of the system and how each depends on the others.

- Trusting and personal relationships among teams and team members.

- Decentralized decision-making authority. Delegation is not enough. Leaders need to share their power and empower team members to make decisions.

- Adaptability. Teams need to be able to pivot and adapt at a second's notice.

- Open sharing of information with everyone.

McChrystal's approach was developed in the course of military intervention in Iraq. Moving all the way to the other end of the political spectrum, we find a remarkably similar set of ideas articulated by anti-nuclear activist and radical feminist, Starhawk. Starhawk makes a distinction between "power-over" and "power-with" leadership. She advocates for "responsive leadership," which is characterized by:

- *Nurturing:* Nurturing leadership skills in others—sharing knowledge, information, skills, experience, and leadership roles;

- *Keeping commitments:* Following through and being accountable to the group;

- *Responding:* Listening, consulting, acting as "an ear, more than a mouth";

- *Transparency:* About information, agendas, power, and reality—even if the news is bad or inconsistent with ideology;

- *Group focus:* Putting the needs of the group and its members before their own;

- *Egalitarianism:* Expecting no special benefits, status, or respect for their leadership position beyond that which all group members receive (Starhawk 1989, 271–272).

We find it inspiring that these two views of effective leadership and team organization, coming from people miles apart ideologically and by life experience, while not identical, are in fact very compatible and express many of the same conclusions about how to achieve systems change.

Trust and Psychological Safety

Amy Edmondson (2019) makes a distinction between trust and psychological safety. Trust is the individual expectation that one can count on another person to do what they promised they would do. Psychological safety is experienced at a group level when people feel safe to speak up, ask questions, suggest ideas, and raise difficult issues without the fear of being marginalized or ridiculed. Social movements require both.

In organizations struggling with dysfunctional internal relationships, the absence of psychological safety is often rampant. This gets expressed in different ways—employees afraid to speak up, people fearful of being alone in the same room with one another, meetings in which only the most trivial issues are raised or where there is no discussion at all, or administrators quick to shut down any discussion of sensitive issues such as race or gender for fear of opening a Pandora's box. Of course, this does not mean that there is no discussion of these issues. These concerns may be widely recognized within the organization or group and even in the broader community, but they are avoided like the plague in open forums.

Narrative Suppression and Microaggressions

In unsafe spaces, leaders are prone to try to control or prevent people from sharing their stories of feeling marginalized or discriminated against or bringing up any conflict at all. In safer spaces, leaders are more likely to try to deal with the situation by naming it, owning it, apologizing if necessary, and taking action to address it. *Narrative suppression* is a means by which people occupying positions of power perpetuate their privileged status, whether intentionally or unconsciously. In healthcare settings, narrative suppression leads to underreporting medical errors causing poorer patient care and worse outcomes.

Many (maybe most) organizational cultures do not support owning up to significant mistakes. There is often a paternalistic tendency to repress information or ignore a problem ostensibly to protect people who are vulnerable from feeling "uncomfortable" or "reminding them of painful experiences." Often this translates to a refusal by leadership or others in privileged positions to acknowledge the bias or discrimination that exists in an organization. Frequently this leads to nondisclosure agreements that can endanger future potential victims. But if we are in constant fear of naming what needs to be changed, there is no way to correct the error. In her book *The Fearless Organization*, Amy Edmonson reports on empirical data that shows teams in which there is openness to reporting mistakes and discussing errors are better at what they do; "The good teams [. . .] don't make more mistakes, they report more" (Edmonson 2019, 10).

As a Latina, I (Jackie) have often been on the receiving end of narrative suppression. This comes in many forms. One of the most common is to wrap dismissive statements in the guise of (not so funny) humor. Some examples from the last few years:

- "For not being an American, your English is pretty good."

- "We need a minority on the committee."

- "You are separate but equal."

- "The US is a melting pot."

- "The natives are restless."

- "She is my startup wife." (A man referring to his wife in a conversation with me.)

And then there are *microaggressions*—small-scale but frequent acts or comments that transmit hostility or are derogatory toward a person or group of people (Sue 2010)—such as raising their voice or speaking slower when I ask for clarification on something they have told me. It never crosses their minds that the information they are delivering lacks clarity. Since they see *me* as the problem, speaking louder and slower will *surely help me understand*.

These statements and behaviors signal that I don't belong, I am unwelcome, and I am "less than." I am keenly aware that, like implicit bias, these statements are not always intentional, but of course at other times, they are clearly purposeful and malicious. Either way, they rarely meet the discrimination threshold that most legal statutes require. Perhaps even more importantly, even if I could meet this threshold and win in court, the underlying causes sustaining the structures of oppression would remain, and I would likely suffer more than the perpetrator. The law is not designed to change systems, it is designed to preserve the status quo and control narratives.

In every organization where these microaggressions occurred, the only option for redress was to file a grievance, an administrative complaint, or proceed with legal action. The opportunities to have conversations around feelings of unbelonging, racism, or misogynism were glaringly missing. As a result, the stories that needed to emerge for systemic change to happen were effectively suppressed. These microaggressions, beyond their impact on me, became woven into the fabric of the organization, normalizing a toxic environment (see also Cohen and Strand 2021).

Allies can interrupt toxic behavior such as microaggressions by publicly naming and rejecting them. Naming behavior creates awareness that microaggressions have taken place and provides opportunities for the aggressors to recognize the negative impact their actions have caused. When allies speak up, they validate the feelings of hurt or confusion those on the receiving end of the microaggression experience, thereby demonstrating that they are not alone and affirming that what they experienced actually did just happen.

Being an ally in this manner can bring its own consequences. I (Bernie) have been told I am too sensitive, have no sense of humor, or have provoked an escalation of the microaggression. But compared to the consequences for the target, this is a pretty small price to pay. Of course, allies do not always come from a position of privilege. For example, when a White employee confronts a manager for treating Black employees with condescension and disrespect, their intervention comes from a place of both privilege and vulnerability. Being an ally always involves some potential negative consequences but for some much more than for others.

We all have a responsibility to react non-defensively and with an open mind when our own behaviors are called out as well. This too can be painful, but the more we understand how hard it is for others to raise this and how important it is to create a climate that is open and accepting for this kind of interaction, the more we will be able to understand these as acts of solidarity rather than hostility.

Creating spaces where people feel psychologically safe enough to have difficult and uncomfortable conversations is not primarily a matter of laws or policies (although those can be important). Actual safe spaces are needed—places where people can go to be protected, heard, and supported and where people are able to hold each other accountable so the hard work necessary to restore damaged relationships can begin.

Safe spaces stem from an organizational culture and leadership that value equity, inclusion, and diversity not just because it is expected but because it is what makes organizations strong, productive, and innovative. Procedures for safe and meaningful reporting of problems are important, but the genuine intention to address problems and to support those who have had the courage to report them is crucial. Developing or reinforcing such a culture requires asking some critical (if complicated) questions, such as:

- How do we support and hold each other accountable?

- How much power do we have and how do we share it?

- What information do we share and how?

- What policies and procedures need to be implemented to ensure that everyone feels safe?

- Where or to whom do we go when we feel unsafe? Where do others go?

- Which emotions are safe to share and which are not? How does this differ by gender, race, sexual identity, etc.?

- How do we hide our feelings of insecurity or vulnerability from others and, more importantly, from ourselves?

- What stops us from sharing?

- What is being said, and not said, when we are together?

- How do we create spaces to celebrate our successes?

- What conversations are happening, or not happening, across groups?

No organization, group, or family provides complete emotional safety. But the effort to do so is nonetheless important. We also have a personal responsibility to let people into our own safe spaces, which is sometimes not so easy.

A Space Invader

When I (Bernie) was a student at Oberlin College, my safe space was *Tank Coop* (a student-run dining hall and dormitory)—safe from political battles, personal struggles, and the general angst of the times (at least mostly so). As were so many of us, I was immersed in efforts to oppose the war in Vietnam along with a range of other causes. By virtue of being president of student government, I was in a leadership position—which meant among other things that in the midst of sit-ins and threats from the administration to expel us, I frequently had to negotiate with hostile college officials.

Shortly after a particularly intense set of actions and negotiations, I was at Tank, when in walked Fred, a student who had led counter-protests in support of the war and who had aggressively forced his way through our picket lines protesting the presence of a Navy Recruiter on campus. He was in my safe space. I flipped out. Why it was there I have no idea, but I grabbed for a toy gun—jumped on a couch and started to pretend to shoot people in the distance and said, "This is what you want to do to Vietnamese peasants and children" or something to that effect. I don't remember exactly what happened next, other than that Fred left. What I soon discovered was that two of my closest friends had invited Fred to Tank to talk about their differences—in an effort to calm things down and see what a personal connection might accomplish. They were none too pleased with me, and I didn't blame them—I was embarrassed. Clearly, I felt the confrontative tensions all around had entered my place of safety at a time when I was very stressed, and I did not react well.

What happened next, several months later, still seems amazing. I was at a political rally, and so was Fred. He hadn't changed his views, but perhaps had softened them.

(Continued)

(*Continued*)

He had just been confronted by other demonstrators. Fred approached me and started to share how hard this was for him. He said, "I don't know why I am telling you this." I certainly didn't either. But I listened, empathized as best I could, and then shared some of my feelings. That was the end of it. I don't remember if we ever talked again or where his journey took him.

I learned a great deal from these interchanges. Every enemy has the potential to be an ally. Our safe spaces are extremely important—but they are not pristine. We have a right to defend them from invasion, but what I was doing was acting out in an arrogant and petulant way. Also I was doing so from a position of privilege and power. Had I been a woman or person of color, my actions would have been viewed very differently and would have had different consequences. My friends were doing good work, and I screwed it up. I still feel bad about it. And yet I must have projected something that allowed Fred to come to me and to talk, and the talk was good.

Can Elites Be Allies for Change?

"Are the winners of our capitalist system—intentionally or not—redefining the world's problems in ways that avoid questioning their own business practices, power, and wealth? Have we lost the essential premise of a just society when we substitute private action by individuals for government policy and public debate?"

(Mark Kramer, "Are the Elite Hijacking Social Change?" *Stanford Social Innovation Review*, Fall 2018, 68)

In 2017, Hurricane María devastated the northeastern part of the Caribbean. Hurricane María was a category 5 storm with winds of 150 mph. In the aftermath many non-governmental organizations and volunteers went to assist Puerto Ricans. There was no electrical power, running water, medicine, food, or many other necessities. Fortunately, those who had food shared it in self-organized community kitchens. Government aid eventually started trickling in but always too little and too late (see also Bonilla 2020).

Eventually, non-governmental organizations started arriving on the island to address some of the immediate needs. When José Andrés came to Puerto Rico to serve millions of meals through his organization World Central Kitchen (WCK), he was labeled a hero. In 2018, he was nominated for a Nobel Peace Prize for his humanitarian work. The WCK website indicates that it "uses the power of food to nourish communities and strengthen economies in times of crisis and beyond." WCK (a not-for-profit non-governmental organization) accepts all kinds of donations, including cryptocurrency (e.g. Bitcoin, Ether, Litecoin). Without wishing to diminish the importance of charity in moments of disaster, we still need to ask whether WCK is a genuine ally for change. WCK receives funding from powerful elites to provide important, immediate relief, but what has it done to advance social change "in times of crisis and beyond"?

Can we advance significant social change by partnering with the elite and those in positions of power? To bring about social change we need to develop connections with both natural allies and with those with whom we have significant differences. This includes those who are in positions of power. And yet these are often the people who have the most to lose if significant change occurs. It is in their best interest to advocate for slow, incremental change, based on existing systems such as the privatization of service delivery, the free market, and charity—the "thousand points of light" in George HW Bush's words.

WCK fed millions of Puerto Ricans, as it has done in many other places where disasters might otherwise have led to mass starvation. For this they should be honored, but these acts of charity do not change the system. As valuable as their work might be, they also enable government leaders to shift responsibility to the private sector; they do not address structural inequalities. On the contrary, they may be perpetuating these through increasing the divide between the haves and have-nots. In Puerto Rico, like many other countries that WCK has served in the past, food inequities and malnourishment persist.

This raises the age-old "Band-Aid" dilemma. Should we be applying bandages to the worst symptoms of inequality, or do we insist on demanding systemic reform and when necessary create new systems? The manifestations of this dilemma are everywhere:

- Should access to justice be achieved by increased legal aid and pro bono representation or by an overhaul of the legal system?

- Do mental health interventions work mainly to help people adapt to an unjust system or do they address the underlying causes of the problems being manifested? (Bernie's father used to ask—"If someone has a rat phobia, do you treat the phobia or get rid of the rats?")

- Do we need more doctors to treat underserved populations, or do we need to restructure the medical system?

- Do we make cars and planes more fuel efficient or do we rethink our whole transportation system and the assumptions behind it?

Of course, the answer is all the above. Treat the phobia and get rid of the rats, and move on to look at the system that resulted in rats being more prevalent in poor communities. But elites are most likely to focus on approaches that are minimally threatening to the systems that have given them their privileged status. So the most system-preserving approaches are the ones that tend to dominate in the absence of profound efforts at social change. Those with power and privilege can be important allies but not if their allegiance is attained at the cost of forgoing the disruptive potential of social movements.

The Need for a Common Purpose

Participants in movements for social change do not need to become best friends or to agree on everything. But they do need to develop a shared vision. Public actions such as demonstrations and rallies are potentially powerful tactics, but they are not the same as organizing sustainable movements for change. We have been part of many groups that have been able to mobilize supporters but have ultimately floundered because of the failure to build a viable organization with a clear vision and common purpose. The Puerto Rico summer of 2019, with its self-organized movement, was able to use mass protests to accomplish its immediate goal of forcing the governor of Puerto Rico to resign. I (Jackie) participated and was inspired and energized by this movement. However, the unjust, corrupt, and colonial government structures in Puerto Rico remain in place.

In her recent book, *The Purpose of Power*, Alicia Garza (2020) distinguishes between popular fronts, which are alliances across a spectrum of political beliefs that come together to accomplish a specific goal, and united fronts, which are long-term alliances among groups who share a strong level of political alignment. For systemic change to occur, a variety of alliances are essential— popular fronts, united fronts, mass movements, and coalitions of many types. We need the energy of unplanned but powerful popular uprisings and the stability of well-organized and durable structures for change. We need on occasion to be willing to work jointly with those who strongly disagree with us and do not share our overall vision but maybe do buy in to a small part of it. People in movements and institutions are complex and have more than "one single story."

Recently, I (Jackie) started working at Eastern Mennonite University (EMU). As I continue to learn about EMU's history, I came across a story that illustrates the power of not falling into a totalizing narrative trap. As a Mennonite faith-based academic institution, EMU adhered to the denomination's stance prohibiting same-sex relationships. Employees in same-sex relationships needed to remain celibate to continue to work at EMU (Brubaker 2019). President Loren Swartzendruber initiated a year-long consultation process that provided an opportunity for the EMU community, including external constituents, to share their stories. In 2015, with the support of the board of trustees, EMU changed its policy. Moving forward, LGBTQIA+ employees can openly be in same-sex relationships and receive the same benefits as those in heterosexual relationships.

In discussions with members of the EMU community, I inquired about the impact of this change on alumni and donor support. After all, for many alumni and donors, this was a significant cultural shift. This policy change could have had a negative financial impact. However, after further conversations with EMU leaders, donors and alumni accepted that EMU was about more than one policy. Most (not all) continued to support the university. Although some alumni and donors disagreed with this change in policy, they continued to support the vision and mission of EMU. The change also attracted new donors. Dialogue freed EMU and its donors from the *single-story* trap.

The Power of Community

The systems sustaining racism, global warming, and misogyny are powerful and resilient. To change them, we need to mobilize the power of community and to organize a network for change that works like a team of teams—in effect a community of communities—a constellation of communities that can support each other in working toward a common goal.

Leaders for change need to foster increased levels of interaction among groups so that new patterns of interactions and relationships emerge. One approach to this is through the creation of *affinity groups*, small, closely knit units dedicated to a common purpose. Affinity groups can become the engines for direct action and can provide safe spaces and support for participants in change efforts. This kind of support can protect and sustain people as they engage in activities that can be risky, even traumatizing, and that can expose people to significant, sometimes violent pushback.

Affinity groups date back at least to mid-19th century and were prominent during the Spanish Civil War in the 1930s. The *tertulias* were small groups (10 to 15 members) of trusted friends opposed to the fascist forces. Their cohesion enhanced their willingness to undertake high-risk actions (Meyer 2007; Snow and Cross 2011). They usually organized in non-hierarchical ways, made decisions by consensus, and worked as closely knit teams. This model of affinity groups was used in antinuclear movements during the 1980s and the Occupy Movements of the 2010s.

Community does not just develop from efforts focused on change. The informal, getting to know each other, having fun part of getting together is also an important part of the glue holding them together. It's one way we learn to be comfortable and to trust (or not trust) each other, and it helps us develop the emotional bonds that can sustain us. During this time of COVID-19 distance, where our group interactions have been so often limited to screen time, we have lost some of this—the time for play, sharing interests, and getting to know each other in multidimensional ways. On the other hand, we have also learned how to develop meaningful relationships over distance and among dispersed participants. The two of us suspect our age demographic is less able to navigate this obstacle to multidimensional interactions as well as those who have grown up relating online. However it is accomplished, communities grow when not all activities are task focused.

Leaders and Boundaries

"Boundaries contain our power so that it can deepen and intensify, and they may keep out what could threaten or disrupt our group. But boundaries may also exclude those who might benefit us or bring us power. A boundary is always, in essence, somewhat arbitrary and false: an island of separation, carved out of the rippling whole."

(Starhawk, *Truth or Dare: Encounters with Power, Authority and Mystery* [San Francisco: Harper Collins Publishing, 1989], 148)

Connecting across differences enables the co-creation of new stories and better understanding, and this can help forge new and potent alliances. But our differences as well as our commonalities need to be respected. Connections are important, and so are boundaries. As a Black woman participating in a cross-racial dialogue shared, "When I say that I want understanding it does not mean that I'm looking for sympathy. I merely want people to know why I'm angry and not to be offended by it" (Tatum 2017, 337).

Organizing for social change requires that we maintain healthy but permeable boundaries. Effective change efforts need to involve many different kinds of people, but they also need to build trust, which is enabled by belonging to a close-knit group. Holding this tension between our need for community and for autonomy—for belonging and yet for safety—is critical to our group identity. As we bring others into our circle of trust and expand it, our collective identity can feel threatened. Leaders who want to work with other groups to advance a cause are some-times viewed as sellouts.

An important challenge for leaders is how to help groups figure out what kind of boundaries they need, how to use each other's strengths, how to share accountability and power, how to deal with intergroup conflicts, and to do all this while maintaining the trust of the group.

Leaders, Followers, Facilitators, and Allies

Building alliances, developing communities, and organizing sys-tems for change requires effective leadership. But what do we mean by leadership? We think of leadership in terms of designated roles and the individuals who fill them. Yet our experience is that regard-less of the formal designation, effective change efforts require that *everyone* take on some of the work traditionally associated with leadership. We all need to be allies, leaders, followers, advocates, mediators, and facilitators. And we all need to do the hard work involved in constructive engagement and strategic disruption. So instead of thinking specifically in terms of leaders, let's consider the leadership tasks that all of us should share responsibility for. These include:

- Engaging directly with conflict; neither avoiding it nor assuming that a solution is always available.

- Focusing on the patterns of interaction that are emerging rather than looking exclusively at individual actions.

- Building relationships with diverse potential allies.

- Being curious.

- Disrupting the system.

- Identifying people to serve as bridges across different social groups.

- Developing constructive approaches for holding each other accountable.

- Fostering "a team of teams."

This is by no means a comprehensive list of what it takes to develop allies, build communities, and create sustainable organizations. The skills necessary to do this lie not within one individual but within the group or community. We all share responsibility for bringing everyone to the leadership table, unleashing each of our potential contributions, and making sure that no one is prevented from being a constructive participant due to rigid leadership structures or exclusionary biases.

Reflective Dialogue: Allies for Change

Bernie: We have been allies through some difficult moments in our work together, Jackie, and I will always be appreciative of that. But I want to focus for a moment on an important ally from across cultures and continents. In the 1990s, Susan Wildau (an important ally herself and one of my partners at CDR) and I worked on a project in Bulgaria to deal with ethnic conflict in the post-Communist era. We had a broad and diverse (Slavic, Christian, Muslim, Turkish, and Roma) set of colleagues in Bulgaria. Our principal partner was Rumen Valchev, the Director of the Open Education Center, who lives in Sofia. Without his leadership and strategic vision, we could not have turned the high-minded ideals behind this effort into a meaningful reality. Describing this effort would require a book itself, but certain things stand out for me about why this was an effective alliance. We disagreed with each other often, sometimes profoundly, but we hung in there because of a commitment to a common vision. We spent considerable time together—planning, problem solving, holding each other to account when necessary, but also visiting, partying, breaking bread, and including each other in our lives in numerous other ways. We respected each other's contributions—we knew that our job was to help provide resources and focus to this effort but that it had to be run by Bulgarians in their way and that not all decisions would be ones we would have made on our own. Rumen was a great ally because he fought with us when necessary, hung out with us, and helped us establish clear but permeable boundaries. Whom do you think of as an important ally?

Jackie: Allies come in all forms and in ways that you least expect. Back in my trial days in Puerto Rico, I had an openly gay client who had been fired from his job. I filed a sex-based discrimination complaint on his behalf. The judge assigned to the case was clearly homophobic and had a reputation of abusing his power. On the first day of the trial, the judge started yelling at me, claiming I had not submitted the pretrial documents, even though I had. He was also making inappropriate insinuations regarding my client's gender identity. I argued strongly on behalf of my client, and the judge threatened me with contempt of court. Then, the opposing counsel stepped in. He confronted the judge, telling him he had no doubts that I had submitted the documents. Opposing counsel and I had respectfully disagreed on many issues throughout the case. And yet, he stepped up as an ally, using his White, straight, male privilege to support my position. He gave his copy of the pretrial documents to the judge, and the counsel and I shared my copy during the remainder of the trial. He also approached my side of the table and offered to support me in any way he could. By checking in to see

(Continued)

(*Continued*)

what I needed and doing so without being condescending or patronizing, he became an ally. He publicly stood in solidarity with me and stood up to a bully. Years later, that judge was removed from the bench and disbarred after being found guilty of domestic violence.

chapter nine

disrupting and connecting for social change: a forward look

Ain't gonna let nobody, turn me 'round.
I'm gonna keep on a-walkin', keep on a-talkin',
Marchin' on to freedom land.

(Civil Rights Movement Song)

Hands to the Heavens, no man, no weapon
Formed against, yes glory is destined
Every day women and men become legends
Sins that go against our skin become blessings
The movement is a rhythm to us
Freedom is like religion to us
Justice is juxtapositionin' us
Justice for all just ain't specific enough
One son died, his spirit is revisitin' us

Truant livin' livin' in us, resistance is us
That's why Rosa sat on the bus
That's why we walk through Ferguson with our hands up
When it go down we woman and man up
They say, "Stay down," and we stand up
Shots, we on the ground, the camera panned up
King pointed to the mountain top and we ran up

(Common, John Legend, and Rymefest. "Glory." On Glory
[from the Motion Picture Selma]. Columbia Records, 2014.)

When the two of us started our journey into the worlds of social movements and conflict engagement, the big new invention was the fax machine. I (Bernie) remember having to run down the street to the office of a friend who had a fax on the few occasions when we actually needed one. Earlier, as an 18-year-old volunteering in the office of CORE (Congress of Racial Equality) in Cleveland, I sometimes felt my most important contribution was understanding how to operate the dodgy mimeograph (Google it if you have no idea what I'm talking about).

Clearly, we live in a very different world today where real-time global communication, instant access to just about whatever information we want, and complex and constantly evolving online networks are an almost unconscious part of many of our lives. To be sure, the degree of access to these is very dependent on privilege, but in one form or another the Internet is available to 60 percent of the world's population (Johnson 2021). How conflict is engaged, constructively or otherwise, and how disruption occurs, strategically or chaotically, has changed immensely over the course of our lifetimes, and any attempt to predict how it will be carried on in the future is fraught and probably foolish.

Yet despite this dramatic evolution, many of the same underlying dynamics regarding engaging in conflict and promoting social change remain. Understanding and addressing the systemic roots of both conflict and exploitation are still essential to social change efforts. Developing flexible, creative, and durable approaches to disrupting entrenched systems of power continues to be a central focus of social movements. But so is the need to negotiate and consolidate gains through electoral, legislative, and legal means and even more importantly through building a growing and more inclusive public consensus about how to move forward. Change efforts require wise leaders, adaptive structures, and broad-based participation. Our capacity to connect across barriers of race, gender, and diversity within our organizations and our communities is essential to our ability to promote progressive change. This was true 100 years ago, remains so today, and is likely to be so in the future.

Throughout this book, we have emphasized the vital importance of a creative mix of engagement, disruption, leadership, and participation. We have also emphasized the powerful and often unrecognized way in which entrenched systems of power resist change. We have looked at this from the point of view of conflict interveners and social activists. These roles offer both complementary and contradictory perspectives. As conflict interveners, we recognize and are committed to the power of bringing people together to explore often extremely divergent viewpoints and to identify potential areas of commonality and agreement. But our background as activists constantly reminds us of the danger of relying exclusively on collaborative approaches when system disruption is essential. Activists need to develop their skills as negotiators and problem solvers and conflict specialists need to heighten their awareness of the dangers of a preoccupation with what can be resolved rather than what must be challenged. The worlds of conflict engagement and social change are much more powerful, sustainable, and effective when they overlap, reinforce, and learn from each other, especially in the face of system resistance.

Conflict Specialists and Social Change; Social Activists and Constructive Engagement

Let's return to Rocky Flats for a second act (the first act was presented in Chapter 7). To review, the Rocky Flats Truth Force was born out of a series of mass actions and sit-ins in 1978 at the Rocky Flats Nuclear Weapons Plant north of Boulder, Colorado. The Truth Force organized sit-ins at Rocky Flats for over a year and was instrumental in forming the Rocky Mountain Peace and Justice Center. But there was indeed a second act (well, actually there have been lots of acts including many other demonstrations, massive industrial fires, FBI raids of the plant, criminal charges against Rockwell International—the plant managers, and huge fines). My (Bernie's) participation in the 1978 actions, and in particular in conducting trainings in nonviolence, peacekeeping, and conflict resolution for activists is what led me into the field of conflict intervention.

After the plant was shut down in 1992, the question of what should be done with the facility became a hot issue. There were concerns about plutonium contamination, safe and appropriate future uses, a proposed link of an interstate highway, and how to make use of an enormous area of undeveloped land in the middle of Boulder and Jefferson Counties. So the US Department of Energy (who owned the facility and was responsible for cleaning it up) decided to convene a stakeholder process to make recommendations about decontaminating the site and appropriate future uses of it. My colleague at CDR Associates, Mary Margaret Golten, was the lead facilitator and organizer of this intense, broad-reaching, and lengthy effort. The outcome was a hard-won and broadly supported consensus among a very diverse group of stakeholders, including members of the Truth Force, local businesses, community members, multiple government agencies, and substantive experts. Today the bulk of the land is a wildlife refuge. The central area where the highest level of plutonium contamination is located is permanently closed to the public, and there is ongoing cleanup and monitoring of the soil and groundwater. The task force had an enormous impact on the decision-making of the responsible governmental agencies about what to do with the site.

Mary Margaret, along with several other partners of CDR Associates, had been active in protests at the plant, but she had not been part of the team that organized them. Because of her long experience as a facilitator and a history of working with many of the agencies involved, she was credible in the role she played. As a participant in anti-nuclear activities, her involvement was reassuring to activists. But she had to earn their trust over and over again throughout this process. She did so by providing a meaningful voice to all participants and respecting everyone's right to make the decisions that they believed best advanced their objectives, even if that made reaching consensual agreements far more difficult.

This conflict-engagement effort helped consolidate the gains made from the years of protests and disruptive actions taken against the plant. The participation of activists who were leaders in their own community was critical in holding the feet of responsible government officials to the fire so that the agreement did not try to cover over the danger of plutonium contamination in the air, soil, and water. Their ongoing attention to what is occurring at the site continues to be critical 30 years after it shut down. Two of the Truth Force founders joined the CDR board of directors. CDR continues to have wide credibility across a broad range of stakeholders. Engagement and disruption reinforced each other throughout these efforts.

Conflict Specialists

Conflict specialists can play important roles in social movements, but to do so, they must be genuinely committed to system change efforts and they need to remain alert to how their work is affecting those efforts. They can do this, for example, by:

- Being effective advocates and negotiators;

- Providing analytic and strategic input to social movements;

- Helping deal with conflicts within and among movements;

- Providing training in conflict engagement to activists when requested to do so—including training in nonviolent social change;

- Assessing the viability and potential of proposed stakeholder processes and helping advocates do the same;

- Coaching advocates on how to handle negotiations and stakeholder dialogues;

- Convening and facilitating those efforts when appropriate;

- Ensuring the participation of activists in relevant engagement processes;

- Advocating for diversity of participation in these processes;

- Promoting a safe, empathic, and respectful space in which difficult conversations can take place;

- Bringing an intersectionality awareness to strategic disruption and constructive engagement efforts;

- Helping to reconcile to the extent possible the tension between chaotic and strategic disruption;

- Helping consolidate the gains of disruption efforts (as at Rocky Flats);

- Conducting restorative justice and other healing efforts to bridge the gap between activists, victims, and perpetrators of injustice where all concerned want genuine healing to occur;

- And more.

Social Activists

Social activists can play an important role in constructive engagement efforts, but they should be clear as to whether such efforts will contribute to their goals and will be carried on in accordance with their fundamental values. They can do this, for example, by:

- Helping conveners conduct situation assessments—analyses of whether engagement efforts should go forward, and if so, under what terms;

- Ensuring that these efforts are about change and not just peace;

- Helping frame the issues in a way that acknowledges immediate objectives without sacrificing long-term goals;

- Advocating for true diversity of participation;

- Staying attentive to the dynamics of intersectionality;

- Building alliances where alliances are possible and can be done with integrity;

- Modeling good listening *and* good advocacy;

- Bringing the emotional dimension of conflict into the process (including anger);

- Building narratives for change that speak to a broad section of participants but also reflect the lived experience of activists;

- Insisting that problems not be sugarcoated, issues not be trivialized, and concerns be heard on their deepest level;

- Looking for creative next steps that move change processes forward. These may include agreements but may also involve further communication and disruption;

- Acting as a liaison between an engagement effort and a larger community;

- Being aware of "agreement fever"—a rush to reaching an agreement even if doing so may not be wise;

- Monitoring agreements to ensure they are being implemented as intended;

- Remaining reflective about one's own actions, attitudes, and feelings;

- Staying open to new ideas and information and asking the same of others;

- Participating in restorative and healing processes that may emerge and that are consistent with social change goals;

- Providing input to conveners, facilitators, and other participants about process, substance, and output;

- Supporting a process with suspicious colleagues if it appears to be a constructive effort;

- And more.

These are not easy tasks for anyone, and it is sometimes best to abandon an effort because it seems too fraught, demanding, or compromising. Conflict specialists need to seek out the participation of social activists who will sometimes make their job more difficult, and leaders of transformative social movements need to consider the potential utility as well as the dangers of taking part in engagement efforts.

The symbiotic relationship between escalating conflict and increasing cooperation is not unique to social change efforts. The interaction between competition and cooperation is a central driver of evolution, human development, and international diplomacy (Mayer 2015; Dawkins 1976). Humans have become the dominant species on earth (for better or worse) because of our ability to cooperate in complex ways (ants are successful for similar reasons) and to adapt. What is often misunderstood, however, is that one thing our cooperative capacity allows us to do is to compete better with other species and with other groups within our own species. As in all arenas of human activity, effective social change efforts require that we embrace the paradoxical codependency of cooperation and competition. Conflict interveners and social activists are natural allies in this effort but not always easy ones. (See Roy et al. 2020 for a conversation between students of conflict resolution and of social movement.)

The Power and Vulnerability of the Status Quo

Change is hard, stagnation impossible. Organic systems must change or they die, but they don't change easily, especially in fundamental ways. Racism has endured for centuries, as has misogyny and imperialism. But these systems of privilege have been forced to adapt to a changing world in which expectations for equality and freedom from oppression have increased significantly. Understanding how we can promote change requires that we understand the power and durability of resistance to it but also the vulnerability of the status quo.

Oppression is sometimes subtle but always harmful. There may be no mass genocides currently occurring in the United States or Canada, but there is mass and disproportionate incarceration of Black, Brown, Indigenous, and Latinx men and women. How domination is exercised has become more sophisticated but still oppressive. In the case of Puerto Rico's colonial relationship with the United States, for example, oppression is based on a system that offers at best partial inclusion but not equity. "In the mid-1900s when Puerto Ricans sought self-determination and sovereignty, they were 'rewarded' with the Commonwealth of Puerto Rico: a system based on partial inclusions and partial rewards" (Font-Guzmán and Alemán 2010, 148). The United States both excluded and included Puerto Ricans by granting them a non-voting representative in the US Congress. The overwhelmingly Black population of Washington, DC, was granted this same half-baked access to power. Oppression also comes through daily acts of aggression that have been normalized and which the oppressed are expected to accept.

Sometimes the hidden resistance is the most entrenched and hardest to overcome. For example, when authorities confront demonstrators with arrests, guns, tear gas, and fire hoses, it is clear what activists are up against. But when the resistance to change comes in the guise of narratives promoted by establishment leaders and the media, it is harder to identify and therefore to fight. The movement for change almost always involves a challenge to the dominant narrative. We see this in virtually every significant arena of conflict. For example:

- Black Lives Matter vs. all lives matter;
- Economic growth vs. environmental sustainability;
- Incremental progress vs. systemic change;
- Protecting the rights of the accused vs. Time's Up;
- Individual freedom vs. justice for the oppressed;
- Public safety vs. defund the police.

None of these represent polar divergences that cannot be dealt with. For example, over time economic growth is only possible with sustainability. Practical steps are a necessary part of system change, but keeping our eyes on the systemic issues involved is essential to ensuring those steps will not further disenfranchise the less powerful.

Conflict engagement and system disruption are both essential to working through these polarities. Disruption raises the systemic problems to a greater level of consciousness and challenges existing power relations. Engagement provides an opportunity to work through our conflicting needs and ideologies and to achieve a broader consensus about the nature of the problem and possible paths forward. But the fundamental mindset that characterizes each approach is very different, and it is therefore hard to take a coordinated approach to engagement and disruption. Engagement efforts almost inevitably promote norms about civility, communication, respect, and finding common ground that are very different (although not necessarily contradictory) from those of determination, courage, confrontation, and clarity of purpose that underly disruption.

This tension is one reason the status quo is so hard to change. It fosters the isolation of social movements and the normalization of approaches to change that are so incremental as to be almost invisible. Another obstacle to change is the enormous resources and immense power of those who benefit from the way things are. The forces aligned against meaningful social change have enormous wealth, control state institutions, dominate the most powerful and established non-governmental institutions such as universities, the media, religious hierarchies, professional organizations, and much more. This allows them to exert power by promoting the view that only small, system-preserving, incremental change is possible.

But realism about the forces arrayed against systemic change ought to be the ally, not enemy, of social movements. Systemic change does happen, and not just by luck. Change happens because the circumstances demand it and people insist on it. Social movements do not succeed in isolation from the structural forces pushing for and resisting change. The protests against the war in Vietnam were prolonged, determined, and multifaceted, but they did not by themselves lead to its end. The fierce resistance of the Vietnamese, the rising death toll of American soldiers (many of whom were drafted), and the growing economic costs were critical factors leading to American withdrawal. But along the way, the resistance to the war in the United States and elsewhere was an important contributing factor. This resistance took many forms. Some were traditionally political, for example, support for antiwar candidates. Some involved continuing public demonstrations—such as mass rallies that attracted upwards of a half million people. There were acts of civil disobedience, and there was violence as well. This mélange came together to lead not only to the end of the fighting but to a change in public attitudes in the United States toward prolonged military engagements (although there are plenty of other ways the United States exerts its military might).

By no means should we minimize the difficulty of system change. Despite the widespread outrage at the murder of George Floyd, there is little evidence that policing of people of color has significantly changed. Sexual violence continues to be rampant and enabled by lax law enforcement and weak institutional responses. Climate change is upon us and its disastrous side effects can be seen everywhere, but actions that actually diminish the sources of global warming are few and far between. But public attitudes are gradually changing, the dominant narratives are slowly evolving, and while we certainly see setbacks (such as in voting rights), the playing field has changed.

OK Boomer: Social Change Across Generations

We are acutely aware that our own experiences and knowledge are in some very important respects dated. We are boomers (Bernie at the front edge, Jackie more toward the end), and along with that comes its own set of implicit biases and constricted visions. Our generation has helped make things worse—and better. So has every previous generation. Generation is itself a questionable, essentializing concept. Our generation(s) fought for and against civil rights, environmental consciousness, military interventions, women's liberation, environmental justice, and the rights of LGBTQIA+ people. We elected conservatives, populists, progressives, and authoritarians.

Each generation has to find its own way, and the biggest mistake we of the boomer era can make is to think we know better about what should happen, what others have experienced, and what is the best path for succeeding generations to take. But that does not mean our voices and experience are irrelevant. Experience and perspective count for something, and yet they can also blind us to the experience and perspective of others. What we know is that social change requires broad and diverse participation, and that includes diversity of age.

We need to feel empowered, no matter our age (or class, gender, ethnicity, or skin color), to lend our voices to engagement and disruption efforts, but we must never assume our voices count for more (or less) than others. Boomers failed to completely clean up the mess left to us by previous generations, and in significant ways we made things worse. We don't have the right to prescribe for others what to do, but we can speak our truths just as we encourage others to.

In writing this book, we are sure that our implicit biases have shown at times, no matter how hard we may have tried to become aware of these. We hope and expect that we will be called out about these and will respond appropriately when that happens. We hope others will do the same. This too is essential to both constructive engagement and strategic disruption.

Truth Telling and Solidarity

Something that unites (or ought to) conflict specialists and social activists is their commitment to truth telling and solidarity. Engagement and disruption are in essence both about sharing truths and bringing people together on the deepest level possible. Both require and provide mechanisms for bearing witness, telling essential stories, working to build the deepest possible connections in the midst of conflict, struggle, and the onslaught of fierce pushback. Conflict engagement processes succeed when they help people say what is most important for them to say and listen fully and receptively to what others have to say.

Disruption is an effort to enter a new perspective and narrative into the dominant framework that has perpetuated an oppressive system. The methods of engagement and disruption are varied and sometimes incompatible, but as we discussed above, the goals can be (and ought to be) reinforcing of each other. For example:

- The LGBTQIA+ communities have provided a powerful lesson in the challenge and rewards of truth telling as a means to assert our right to be true to who we are. Coming out is an act of truth telling and reaching out for solidarity. It is also an act of disruption and vulnerability.

- Second-wave feminism made extensive use of "consciousness raising groups" in the 1960s and 1970s. The focus of these groups was on the experiences of women as individuals and as a group in a patriarchal society. Members told their own stories and listened to those of others, and in doing so developed a sense of solidarity that was essential to building a movement.

- The #MeToo movement has encouraged survivors of sexual abuse to tell their stories and in so doing to gain strength, validation, and solidarity from other survivors and their supporters.

- Black Lives Matter has brought the issue of state oppression of BIPOC communities to the fore by highlighting spectacular instances of violence against people of color and insisting that their stories be told and that they be remembered.

- Every day there seems to be new studies documenting the severity of the climate crisis we face and examples of extremely troubling patterns of floods, drought, fire, and new temperature records—both hot and cold.

The onslaught of global stories can be overwhelming and that is why some of the most influential ones relate the effect of climate change on individuals or on small communities—such as the burning of Lytton, British Columbia, after it recorded the hottest temperature in Canadian history or the story of individual farmers going bankrupt or losing their entire livestock due to draught.

- Truth and reconciliation processes have taken place in many societies emerging from oppressive and even genocidal experiences. Most notably, the Truth and Reconciliation Commission in South Africa but also in places as varied as Canada in relationship to the Indian Residential Schools, in Rwanda subsequent to the genocidal warfare of the early 1990s, and in Australia in regard to long-standing discrimination against Aboriginals and Pacific Islanders. The premise of these efforts is that providing an opportunity for people to tell their stories, when connected with appropriate measures to correct the underlying oppression they reveal, will produce healing and a stronger sense of community.

These efforts are not straightforward roads to system change, and if they are about reconciliation but not change, they can actually perpetuate a problem. But when the engagement efforts are also about disruption, they can have an enormous impact.

We should be careful not to minimize the toll that sharing these stories takes on victims of oppression. Storytelling is imperfect and sometimes hurtful. Storytelling can be an act of necessity as well as bravery. The burden of oppression becomes intolerable, and the need to tell stories becomes essential for survival. And when the oppressed finally share their stories, they are often met with dismissive responses. For example, they may be told, implicitly or directly, how they are expected to behave or to conform to stereotypical ideas of how a queer person, Latina woman, or Black woman is "supposed" to act. A non-oppressive system is one in which people share their story for the joy of sharing, learning, and connecting with others and not as a survival mechanism.

Each of the examples above involved pain as well as healing, and each was flawed in its own way. The consciousness-raising groups of second-wave feminism were largely composed of straight, White, middle-class women. The South African Truth and Reconciliation Commission gave many victims of apartheid an opportunity to be heard, but the restitution that was supposed to follow was woefully inadequate. Nonetheless, the truth-telling efforts were essential to social change, imperfect though they might have been.

Finding Sustenance in Struggle

"Don't mourn, organize!"
—*Joe Hill, Labor activist, just prior to his execution on trumped-up murder charges, 1915*

We ended the first and fifth chapters of this book with reflections on what has kept us going as both activists and conflict intervention practitioners. As we near the end of the final chapter, we again consider what sustains us. For both of us, the struggle to build a better world is not only a moral obligation but a life-giving endeavor. We believe that to be the case for just about everyone engaged in long-term struggles for change whether focusing on constructive engagement, system disruption, or both. So we ask again of each of us, what sustains and inspires us as we engage in efforts to both disrupt and connect?

Reflective Dialogue: The life giving energy of social struggle
Jackie: For me, it has always been about service—a mutual experience of giving and receiving gratitude. How through service, what appears to be an insignificant act of kindness

has the potential of spreading through a system in unimaginable ways.

I have learned that in unequal and oppressive systems, building relationships across differences, connecting with each other's humanity, building community, and exercising "active patience" (as my mother used to say) are revolutionary and disruptive. Active patience does not mean passivity. We can patiently wait for change to happen, as we organize, build alliances, and when necessary, escalate. Those who sustain oppressive systems fear emotions such as anger and kindness more than violence. Emotions are the threads that weave us into solidarity with each other. Solidarity facilitates speaking truth to power. Perhaps this is why most conflict resolution models (e.g. negotiation, mediation) in the Western world want us to be rational and suppress emotions. What better way to maintain an oppressive status quo than by keeping agents of social change from being in solidarity with each other?

I have experienced the power of what can happen when a few good people get together and start a conversation. It is how we begin to organize and plan for change. Talking is how naming oppression and framing our narrative takes place. It is how we build solidarity and respect with each other, despite our differences. It is energizing to build bridges across differences and strategize ways of transforming systems so that they work for everyone and not just a few.

Bernie: I have not always been able to maintain a consistent presence as a social activist because, unlike my work as a conflict intervener, activism did not come wrapped up as a job, with a clear organizational structure, formal accountability systems, and not insignificantly, a salary. That did not mean that the activist part of my life disappeared, because I continued to participate in many ways—for example, as a

(Continued)

(*Continued*)

writer, a board member of an environmental organization, by attending demonstrations, and by helping movement groups with internal conflicts or planning processes. But as with many of us, there have been ups and downs in my level of involvement. Some of this has had to do with my stage in life. Raising young children, trying to build a business, and reassessing some of the excesses of my youthful certainties changed my priorities to some extent—although not my basic values.

What has remained a constant is the sense of fulfillment that I have felt when I was thoroughly engaged in both engagement and disruption efforts, when I experienced the power of these two sides of the coin of social change. I have also found it energizing to allow myself to give voice to both the analytical and emotional sides of my approach to social issues. I hope my ability to connect with people, even those I do not agree with, has withstood the test of these polarizing times, and that my willingness to speak my truth in a meaningful way has also endured through the years of being mostly focused on helping others to speak theirs. I am sure that my record on this has its share of blemishes but also some important successes. I have tried to bring both these elements into this book.

One of life's most fulfilling experiences, for me at least, is finding that zone where I am able to connect, to listen, to discuss, to speak my truth, to express empathy for the truths of others, to call out behavior that is not acceptable, and to look for ways to build constructive relationships across differences. Achieving that place is not easy, but the search for it has given tremendous meaning to my life, and that meaning is what sustains me. As I slowly adopt the mantle of being "retired" and an "elder," I am in some ways better able to undertake that search, but it has always been there as a defining characteristic of what makes me tick.

Remember George Floyd

"We each need the memory of the other . . . and . . . if
we want to share the beauty of the world, if we want
to show solidarity in its suffering, we have to learn to
remember together."
(Édouard Glissant, *Poetics of Relation*
[Ann Arbor: University of Michigan Press, 1997])

The ideas in this book have been percolating for a long time,
but what finally precipitated our decision to enter on this venture
was the murder of George Floyd. The graphic video of what happened to him coalesced so many wrongs into a clear story and gal-
vanized so many of us to up the ante of our activism. It also posed
the challenge of figuring out how to carry on a productive conflict
in our communities about White supremacy and institutional racism. Systems needed to be disrupted, conflict needed to be engaged
in, change needed to happen. This is an old story but one for the
future as well.

Remembering George Floyd is about remembering Trayvon
Martin, Eric Garner, Tamir Rice, Michael Brown, Ahmaud Arbery,
and so many more. It is about remembering Matthew Shepard,
Sarah Everard, and the thousands of women and LGBTQIA+ people who have been murdered or destroyed. It is about remembering
the fate of people around the world who are or will be victims of
human-caused climate change. It is about remembering those subjected to colonialism, anti-Semitism, and Islamophobia reaching
back generations and continuing today.

If we remember, we will act. If we act with compassion, determination, wisdom, and courage, we can change the world.

references

Abeijón, Matías. "El poder y el sujeto: Sujeción, norma y resistencia en Judith Butler." In *El Sujeto en Cuestión*, Pedro Karczmarczyk (Ed.). Buenos Aires: Universidad Nacional de La Plata, 2014.

Adichie, Chimamanda Ngozi. "The Danger of a Single Story." TED Global video, filmed July 2009, 18:34. https://www.ted.com/talks/chimamanda_ngozi_adichie_the_danger_of_a_single_story?language=en#t-2214.

Allred, Keith G. "Anger and Retaliation in Conflict: The Role of Attribution," *The Handbook of Conflict Resolution: Theory and Practice*, Peter T. Coleman, Morton Deutsch, and Eric C. Marcus (Eds.). San Francisco: Jossey-Bass, 2000, 236–255.

Almanac Singers, The. "Talking Union and other Union Songs (liner notes)." Washington, DC: Folkways Records, 1955.

Alter, Charlotte, Suyin Hayes, and Justin Worland. "2019 Person of the Year: Greta Thunberg." *Time* magazine, December 23/30, 2019. https://time.com/person-of-the-year-2019-greta-thunberg/.

American Medical Association. "The commission to end health care disparities: Unifying efforts to achieve quality care for all Americans." USA: American Medical Association, 2009.

Anzaldúa, Gloria. *Borderlands La Frontera: The New Mestiza.* San Francisco, CA: Aunt Lute Books, 1999.

Associated Press. "Navy Resumes Vieques Exercises Despite Pleas from Opponents." *The New York Times*, August 3, 2001, sec. A.

Atewologun, Doyin. "Intersectionality Theory and Practice," *Oxford Research Encyclopedias, Business and Management*, 2018. https://oxfordre.com/business/view/10.1093/acrefore/9780190224851.001.0001/acrefore-9780190224851-e-48.

Banaji, Mahzarin R., and Anthony G. Greenwald. *Blindspots: Hidden Biases of Good People*. New York: Delacorte Press. 2013.

Begnaud, David. "David Begnaud reflects on Hurricane Maria coverage," CBS News, YouTube, June 9, 2018. https://www.youtube.com/watch?v=9Jl4VCrrYC8.

Berkley, Andrew, and John Letzing. "The legacy of 'redlining'. How earlier urban zoning reinforces racial segregation." *World Economic Forum*, July 2, 2020. https://www.weforum.org/agenda/2020/07/how-redlining-remains-a-source-of-racial-injustice/.

Blackstock, Cindy. "Screaming Into Silence," *Maclean's*, June 30, 2021. https://www.macleans.ca/opinion/residential-schools-survivors-cindy-blackstock/.

Blum, Beth. "The Radical History of Corporate Sensitivity Training," *The New Yorker*, September 24, 2020. https://www.newyorker.com/culture/cultural-comment/the-radical-history-of-corporate-sensitivity-training.

Blystad, Astrid., Haldis Haukanes, Getnet Tadele, and Karen Marie Moland. "Reproductive health and the politics of abortion," *International Journal for Equity in Health*, 19, no. 39 (2020). https://doi.org/10.1186/s12939-020-1157-1.

Bonilla, Yarimar. "The coloniality of disaster: Race, empire, and the temporal logics of emergency in Puerto Rico, USA," *Political Geography*, vol. 78 (April 2020). https://doi.org/10.1016/j.polgeo.2020.102181.

Bonilla, Yarimar, and Marisol Lebrón. *Aftershocks of Disaster: Puerto Rico Before and After the Storm*. Chicago: Haymarket Books, 2019.

Bowen, Murray. *Family Therapy and Clinical Practice*. Lanham: Rowman and Littlefield Publishers Inc., 1985.

Bradlee, Ben Jr. *The Forgotten: How the People of One Pennsylvania County Elected Donald Trump and Changed America*. New York: Little, Brown, and Co., 2018.

Bramble, Linda. "What Is at the Heart of Creative Dialogue." *Leading Creatively*, June 18, 2017. http://www.leadingcreativitycreatively.com/what-is-at-the-heart-of-creative-dialogue.

Brubaker, David R., Everett N. Brubaker, Carolyn E. Yoder, and Teresa J. Haase. *When The Center Does Not Hold: Leading in an Age of Polarization*. Minneapolis, MN: Fortress Press, 2019.

Brune, Michael. "Pulling Down Our Monuments," *Sierra Club Website*, July 22, 2020. https://www.sierraclub.org/michael-brune/2020/07/john-muir-early-history-sierra-club.

Bump, Phillip. "The Fix," *The New York Times*, August 31, 2016.

Bush, Robert A Baruch, and Joseph P. Folger. *The Promise of Mediation: Responding to Conflict Through Empowerment and Recognition*. San Francisco: Jossey-Bass, 2005.

Butler, Judith. *Cuerpos que importan*. Buenos Aires, Argentina: Paídos, 1993.

Chenoweth, Erica, and Maria J. Stephan. *Why Civil Resistance Works: The Strategic Logic of Nonviolent Conflict*. New York: Columbia University Press, 2011.

Cloke, Kenneth. *Mediating Dangerously: The Frontiers of Conflict Resolution*. San Francisco: Jossey-Bass/Wiley, 2001.

Cloke, Kenneth. "10 Actions We Can Take to Turn Adversarial, Autocratic, Power-Based Political Conflicts into Collaborative, Democratic, Interest-Based Social Problem Solving." Mediation.com, January 2021. https://www.mediate.com/articles/cloke-10-actions.cfm.

Cohen, Adam. *Supreme Inequality: The Supreme Court's Fifty-Year Battle for a more Unjust America*. New York, New York: Penguin Press, 2020.

Cohen, Claudia E., and Palma Joy Strand. "Microaggressions and Macro-Injustices: How Everyday Interactions Reinforce and Perpetuate Social Systems of Dominance and Oppression." 2021. Article on file with author.

Coleman, Peter T. "Power and Conflict," *The Handbook of Conflict Resolution: Theory and Practice.* Morton Deutsch and Peter T. Coleman, (Eds.). San Francisco: Jossey-Bass/Wiley, (2000), pp. 120–143.

Coleman Peter T., Antony G. Hacking, Mark A. Stover, Beth Fisher-Yoshida, and Andrzej Nowak. "Reconstructing Ripeness I: A Study of Constructive Engagement in Protracted Social Conflicts," *Conflict Resolution Quarterly*, vol. 26, no. 1 (Fall 2008) doi:10.1002/crq.222.

Crenshaw, Kimberle. "Demarginalizing the Intersection of Race and Sex: A Black Feminist Critique of Antidiscrimination Doctrine, Feminist Theory and Antiracist Politics," *University of Chicago Legal Forum.* Vol. 1989, Issue 1, Article 8. (1989): 139–167.

Dawkins, Richard. *The Selfish Gene.* New York: Oxford University Press, 1976.

Deese, Kaelan. "Utah, Nebraska voters approve measures stripping slavery language from state constitutions," *The Hill*, November 4, 2020. https://thehill.com/homenews/state-watch/524469-utah-nebraska-voters-approve-measure-stripping-slavery-language-in.

Delgado, Richard, and Jean Stefancic. *Critical Race Theory: An Introduction.* New York: New York University Press, 2012.

Della Noce, Dorothy. "Seeing Theory in Practice: Analysis of Empathy in Mediation," *Negotiation Journal*, 15, no.3 (July 1999): 271–301.

Democratic Socialists of America. "What Is Democratic Socialism?" accessed November 15, 2020. https://www.dsausa.org/about-us/what-is-democratic-socialism/.

Docherty, Jayne Seminare. *Learning Lessons from Waco: When the Parties Bring Their Gods to the Negotiation Table.* Syracuse, New York: Syracuse University Press, 2001.

Edmondson, Amy C. *The Fearless Organization: Creating Psychological Safety in the Workplace for Learning, Innovation, and Growth.* Hoboken, NJ: John Wiley & Sons, Inc., 2019.

Elliott, Justin. "Reagan's embrace of apartheid South Africa," *Salon*, February 5, 2011. https://www.salon.com/2011/02/05/ronald_reagan_apartheid_south_africa.

Erikson, Erik H. *Gandhi's Truth: On the Origins of Militant Nonviolence.* New York: W.W. Norton & Company Inc., 1969.

Fannon, Frantz. *The Wretched of the Earth.* New York, NY: Grove Press, 1963.

Finkelman, Paul. "Master John Marshall and the Problem of Slavery," *The University of Chicago Law Review Online*, August 31, 2020. https://lawreviewblog.uchicago.edu/2020/08/31/marshall-slavery-pt1/.

Flagg, Martha. "Is There a Connection Between Undocumented Immigrants and Crime?" *The New York Times*, May 15, 2019.

Floyd, Philonise. "George Floyd's brother reacts to Chauvin Guilty verdict," *CNN Interview*, April 20, 2021. https://www.cnn.com/videos/us/2021/04/20/philonise-floyd-george-brother-verdict-guilty-derek-chauvin-trial-sot-vpx.cnn/video/playlists/derek-chauvin-trial-for-george-floyds-death/.

Font-Guzmán, Jacqueline N. *Experiencing Puerto Rican Citizenship and Cultural Nationalism.* New York: Palgrave Macmillan, 2015.

Font-Guzmán, Jacqueline N. "Puerto Ricans are hardly U.S. citizens. They are colonial subjects," *The Washington Post*, December 13, 2017a.

Font-Guzmán, Jacqueline N. "Personal Reflection on 50 Years of Loving: Creating Spaces of Differences by Demanding 'The Right to Opacity,'" *Creighton Law Review*, 50 no. 3, (2017): 637–640.

Font-Guzmán, Jacqueline N. "How a Puerto Rican Woman Ended Up in a Field Dominated by Anglo Men," Nancy Welsh and Howard Gadlin (Eds.), *Evolution of a Field: Personal Histories in Conflict Resolution.* Saint Paul: DRI Press, 2020.

Font-Guzmán, Jacqueline N., and Yanira Alemán. "Human Rights Violations in Puerto Rico: Agency from the Margins," *Journal of Law and Social Challenges*, 12 (2010): 107–149.

García, Sandra E. "The Woman Who Created #MeToo Long Before Hashtags," *The New York Times*, October 20, 2017. https://www.nytimes.com/2017/10/20/us/me-too-movement-tarana-burke.html.

Garza, Alicia. *The Purpose of Power: How We Come Together When We Fall Down*. New York, NY: One World, 2020.

Gerardi, Deborah. "Conflict Engagement: Workplace Dynamics," *American Journal on Nursing*, 115, no. 4 (2015).

Gibran, Kahlil. *The Prophet*. New York, NY: Alfred A. Knopf, 1960.

Giridharadas, Anand. *Winners Take All: The Elite Charade of Changing the World*. New York: Knopf, 2018.

Gleick, James. *Chaos: Making a New Science*. New York: The Penguin Group, 2008.

Glissant, Édouard. *Poetics of Relation*. Ann Arbor: University of Michigan Press, 1997.

Goleman, Daniel. "Bruno Bettelheim Dies at 86," *The New York Times*, March 14, 1990.

Gramsci, Antonio. "Letters from Prison" quoted in Frank Rosengarten, *The Revolutionary Marxism of Antonio Gramsci*. Brill, 2013.

Hadfield, Gillian (@ghadfield). Twitter, January 29, 2018. https://twitter.com/ghadfield/status/958162767504031744.

Hagan, Lisa. "Trump to Coal Industry: 'Election Is Last Shot for Miners,'" *The Hill*, August 10, 2016. https://thehill.com/blogs/ballot-box/presidential-races/291041-trump-to-coal-country-this-election-is-the-last-shot-for.

Haley, Jay. *Problem Solving Therapy*. San Francisco: Jossey-Bass, 1987.

History.com editors. "Salt March," January 16, 2020. https://www.history.com/topics/india/salt-march.

Hoffman, Kelly M., Sophie Trawalter, Jordan R. Axt, and M. Norman Oliver. "Racial bias in pain assessment and treatment recommendations, and false beliefs about biological differences between blacks and whites," *PNAS*, 113, no. 16 (April 19, 2016): 4296–4301.

Horsley, Scott. "Fact Check: Hillary Clinton and Coal Mining Jobs," NPR *Political Newsletter*, May 3, 2016. https://www.npr.org/2016/05/03/476485650/fact-check-hillary-clinton-and-coal-jobs.

Houston-Edwards, Kelsey. "The Math of Making Connections," *Scientific American*, April 2021, pp. 22–29.

Immerwahr, Daniel. *How to Hide an Empire: A History of the Greater United States*. New York: Farrar, Strauss, and Giroux, 2019.

Institute of Medicine of the National Academies (IOMNA). *Unequal treatment: Confronting racial and ethnic disparities in health care*. Washington, DC: The National Academy Press, 2002.

Johnson, Alexis McGill. "I'm the Head of Planned Parenthood. We're Done Making Excuses for Our Founder," *The New York Times* (online), April 17, 2021a. https://www.nytimes.com/2021/04/17/opinion/planned-parenthood-margaret-sanger.html.

Johnson, Joseph. "Global Digital Population as of January 2021," *Statista*, September 10, 2021b. https://www.statista.com/statistics/617136/digital-population-worldwide/.

Jones, Rachel K., Elizabeth Witwer, and Jenna Jerman. *Abortion Incidence and Service Availability in the United States, 2017*. Guttmacher Institute, New York: 2019, https://www.guttmacher.org/report/abortion-incidence-service-availability-us-2017.

Kahneman, Daniel, and Amos Tversky. "Prospect Theory: An Analysis of Decision Making Under Risk," *Handbook of the Fundamentals of Financial Decision Making*. Maclean, Leonard C., and William T. Zeimba (Eds.). Singapore: World Scientific Publishing Company, 2013.

Keenan, James. "Support for same sex marriage is proof that culture wars do end," *The Toronto Star*, June 20, 2021. https://www.thestar.com/news/world/2021/06/20/support-for-same-sex-marriage-is-proof-that-culture-wars-do-end.html.

Kendi, Ibram X. *How to Be an Antiracist*. New York: One World, 2019.

The King Center. "The King Philosophy – Nonviolence365," accessed August 11, 2021. https://thekingcenter.org/about-tkc/the-king-philosophy/.

Kishore, Nishant, Domingo Marqués, Ayesha Mahmud, Mathew V. Kiang, Irmary Rodríguez, Arian Fuller, Peggy Ebner, Cecilia Sorensen, Fabio Racy, Jay Lemery, Leslie Maas, Jennifer Leaning, Rafael Irizarry, Satchit Balsari, and Caroline O. Buckee. "Mortality in Puerto Rico After Hurricane María," *The New England Journal of Medicine*, 379 no. 2 (2018): 162–170.

Klain, Hannah, Kevin Morris, and Rebecca Ayala. "Waiting to Vote, Racial Disparities in Election Day Experiences," *Brennan Center for Justice*, June 3, 2020. https://www.brennancenter.org/sites/default/files/2020-06/6_02_WaitingtoVote_FINAL.pdf.

Klein, Ezra. *Why We're Polarized*. New York: Avid Reader Press, 2020.

Klein, Ezra. "Transcript: Ezra Klein Interviews Natalie Wynn and Will Wilkinson," *The Ezra Klein Show*, NYTimes.com, April 27, 2021. https://www.nytimes.com/2021/04/27/podcasts/ezra-klein-podcast-cancel-culture-transcript.html.

Kottler, Jeffrey A. *What You Don't Know About Leadership But Probably Should*. New York: Oxford University Press, 2018.

Kramer, Mark. "Are the Elite Hijacking Social Change?" *Stanford Social Innovation Review*, Fall, 2018. https://ssir.org/books/reviews/entry/are_the_elite_hijacking_social_change.

Krugman, Paul. "Getting Real About Coal and Climate," *The New York Times*, April 22, 2021. https://www.nytimes.com/2021/04/22/opinion/coal-mine-workers-climate.html.

Kuhn, Thomas S. *The Structure of Scientific Revolutions*, 3rd ed. Chicago: The University of Chicago Press, 1996.

Lande, John. "ADR's Place in Navigating a Polarized Era," *Indisputably.org*, February 16, 2021. http://indisputably.org/2021/02/adrs-place-in-navigating-a-polarized-era.

Lasch-Quinn, Elizabeth. *Race Experts: How Racial Etiquette, Sensitivity Training, and New Age Therapy Hijacked the Civil Rights Revolution.* New York: W.W. Norton and Co., 2001.

Lederach, John Paul. *The Moral Imagination: The Art and Soul of Building Peace.* New York: Oxford University Press, 2005.

Lenin, Vladimir Ilyich. "Experience of the Paris Commune of 1871. Marx's Analysis," *The State and Revolution.* https://www.marxists.org/archive/lenin/works/1917/staterev/ch03.htm.

Lepore, Jill. *These Truths: A History of the United States.* New York: WW. Norton & Company, 2018.

Lind, Michael. *The New Class War: Saving Democracy from the Managerial Elite.* New York: Penguin Random House, 2020.

Lorde, Audre. *Your Silence Will Not Protect You.* UK: Silver Press, 2017.

Macfarlane, Julie. "The National Self-Represented Litigants Project: Identifying and Meeting the Needs of Self-Represented Litigants: Final Report," The National Self-Represented Litigants Project, May 2013. https://representingyourselfcanada.com/wp-content/uploads/2016/09/srlreportfinal.pdf.

Macfarlane, Julie. *Going Public: A Survivor's Journey from Grief to Action.* Toronto: Between the Lines, 2020.

Mandela, Nelson. "I Am Prepared to Die." The Nelson Mandela Archives, accessed August 11, 2021. http://db.nelsonmandela.org/speeches/pub_view.asp?pg=item&ItemID=NMS010&txtstr=prepared%20to%20die.

Martin, Emily. *Flexible Bodies: The role of immunity in American culture from the days of polio to the age of AIDS.* Boston: Beacon Press, 1994.

Matthews, David. "Anderson Cooper regrets comparing Trump to 'obese turtle' during election coverage," *New York Daily News*, November 8, 2020. https://www.nydailynews.com/news/national/ny-anderson-cooper-regret-election-night-trump-obese-turtle-20201108-dfgnm7ycajep7pdxiwybb4jr5i-story.html.

Maxwell, Angie. "What We Get Wrong About the Southern Strategy," *The Washington Post,* July 26, 2019.

Mayer, Bernard. *Beyond Neutrality: Confronting the Crisis in Conflict Resolution.* San Francisco: Jossey-Bass, 2004.

Mayer, Bernard. *Staying with Conflict: A Strategic Approach to Ongoing Disputes.* San Francisco: Jossey-Bass, 2009.

Mayer, Bernard. *The Dynamics of Conflict: A Guide to Engagement and Resolution*, 2nd ed. San Francisco: Jossey-Bass, 2012.

Mayer, Bernard. "What We Talk About When We Talk About Neutrality: A Commentary on the Susskind—Stulberg Debate, 2011 Edition," *Marquette Law Review*, 95, no. 3 (Spring 2012).

Mayer, Bernard. *The Conflict Paradox: Seven Dilemmas at the Core of Disputes.* San Francisco: Jossey-Bass, 2015.

Mayer, Bernard. "Are We Ever Neutral? Should We Be?" *ACResolution Magazine,* January 2018, 19.

McCaffrey, Katherine. *Military Power and Popular Protest: The U.S. Navy in Vieques, Puerto Rico.* New Brunswick: Rutgers University Press, 2002.

McChrystal, Stanley, Tantum Collins, David Silverman, and Chris Fussell. *Team of Teams: New Rules of Engagement for a Complex World.* US: Penguin Random House, 2015.

Memmi, Albert. *Dominated Man: Notes toward a portrait.* New York: Onion Press. 1968.

Menakem, Resmaa. *My Grandmother's Hands: Racialized Trauma and the Pathway to Mending our Hearts and Bodies.* Las Vegas: Central Recovery Press, 2017.

Meyer, David. *The Politics of Protest: Social Movements in America.* New York: Oxford University Press, 2007.

Minuchin, Salvador. *Families and Family Therapy.* Cambridge: Harvard University Press, 1974.

Nash, Ronald H. *Worldviews in Conflict: Choosing Christianity in a World of Ideas.* Grand Rapids: Zondervan Publishing House, 1992.

NC Department of Natural and Cultural Resources. "Ella Baker: Did You Know...," October 26, 2017. https://www.ncdcr.gov/blog/2017/10/26/ella-baker-did-you-know.

Ocasio-Cortez, Alexandria. 2021. "What Happened at the Capitol." Instagram, February 2, 2021. https://www.instagram.com/tv/CKxlyx4g-Yb/.

Page, Scott. *The Difference: How the Power of Diversity Creates Better Groups, Firms, Schools, and Societies*. Princeton: Princeton University Press, 2007.

Pascale, Richard T., Mark Millemann, and Linda Gioja. *Surfing the Edge of Chaos: The Laws of Nature and The New Laws of Business*. New York: Three Rivers Press, 2000.

Perea, Juan F. "Fulfilling Manifest Destiny: Conquest, Race, and the Insular Cases," in *Foreign in a Domestic Sense: Puerto Rico, American Expansion, and the Constitution*. Durham: Duke University Press, 2001, p. 140.

Pettigrew, Thomas F., "Social Psychological Perspectives on Trump Supporters," *Journal of Social and Political Psychology* 5, no. 1, (2017): 107–116.

Pew Research Center. "Attitudes Toward Same Sex Marriage," May 14, 2019. https://www.pewforum.org/fact-sheet/changing-attitudes-on-gay-marriage/.

Politico staff. "Full text: Donald Trump 2016 RNC draft speech transcript," *Politico.com*, July 21, 2016. https://www.politico.com/story/2016/07/full-transcript-donald-trump-nomination-acceptance-speech-at-rnc-225974.

Pulitzer Prize Special Citations and Awards. "Special Citation to Darnella Frazier." *Pulitzer Prizes*. https://www.pulitzer.org/prize-winners-by-category/260 (accessed June 16, 2021).

Putnam, Robert D. "E Pluribus Unum: Diversity and Community in the Twenty-First Century. The 2006 Johan Skytte Prize Lecture," *Scandinavian Political Studies*, 30, no. 2 (2007): 137–174.

Pyke, Karen D. "What Is Internalized Racial Oppression and Why Don't We Study It? Acknowledging Racism's Hidden Injuries," *Sociological Perspectives*, 53, no. 4 (December 2010): 551–572.

Reagan, Ronald. "Inaugural address, January 20,1981," *The Ronald Reagan Presidential Foundation and Institute*. https://www .reaganfoundation.org/ronald-reagan/reagan-quotes-speeches/ inaugural-address.

Rinaldi, Matthew. *Fire at the Freedom House: A Civil Rights Memoir*. Matthew Rinaldi, 2021.

Rothman, Jay. *Resolving Identity Based Conflict in Nations, Organizations, and Communities*. San Francisco: Jossey-Bass, 1997.

Rothstein, Richard. *The Color of Law: A Forgotten History of How Our Government Segregated America*. New York: Liveright Publishing Corporation, 2017.

Roy, Beth, John Burdick, and Louis Kriesberg. "A Conversation Between Conflict Resolution and Social Movement Scholars," *Conflict Resolution Quarterly*, 27, no. 4 (Summer 2010): 347–368.

Samuels, Alex, Elena Mejía, and Nathaniel Rakich. "The States Where Efforts to Restrict Voting Are Escalating," *FiveThirtyEight*, March 29, 2021. https://fivethirtyeight.com/features/ the-states-where-efforts-to-restrict-voting-are-escalating.

Saner, Emine. "Interview: Zelda Perkins: 'There will always be men like Weinstein. All I can do is try to change the system that enables them,'" *The Guardian*, December 23, 2020. https://www .theguardian.com/world/2020/dec/23/zelda-perkins-there-will- always-be-men-like-weinstein-all-i-can-do-is-try-to-change- the-system-that-enables-them.

Saunders, George. *Lincoln in the Bardo*. New York: Random House, 2017.

Saunders, George. *A Swim in a Pond in the Rain; In Which Four Russians Give a Master Class on Writing, Reading, and Life*. New York: Random House, 2021.

Sharp, Gene. *The Politics of Nonviolent Action (3 vols.)*. Westford: Porter Sargent Publishers, 1973.

Smith, Zadie. *Feel Free: Essays*. New York: Penguin Press, 2018.

Snow, David. A, and Remy Cross. "Radicalism within the Context of Social Movements: Processes and Types," *Journal of Strategic Security* 4, no. 4 (Winter 2011): 115–130.

Starhawk. *Truth or Dare: Encounters with Power, Authority and Mystery*. San Francisco: Harper Collins Publishing, 1989.

Stobbs, Nigel. "The nature of juristic paradigms: Exploring the theoretical and conceptual relationship between adversarialism and therapeutic jurisprudence," *Washington University Jurisprudence Review*, 4 no. 1 (2011): 97–150.

Strand, Palma Joy. "The Civic Underpinnings of Legal Change: Gay Rights, Abortion, and Gun Control," *Temple Political & Civil Rights Law Review*, 21, no. 1 (2011): 117–162.

Strand, Palma Joy. "Mirror, Mirror, on the Wall...: Reflections on Fairness and Housing in the Omaha-Council Bluffs Region," *Creighton Law Review*, 50 (2017): 183–247.

Sue, Derald Wing. *Microaggressions in Everyday Life: Race, Gender, and Sexual Orientation*. New Jersey: John Wiley & Sons, 2010.

Tatum, Beverly Daniel. *Why Are All the Black Kids Sitting Together in the Cafeteria? And other conversations about race*. New York, NY: Basic Books, 2017.

Taub, Amanda. "The unsexy truth about why the Arab Spring failed," *Vox*, January 27, 2016. https://www.vox.com/2016/1/27/10845114/arab-spring-failure.

Taylor, Derrick Bryson. "George Floyd Protests: A Timeline," *The New York Times*, March 28, 2021. https://www.nytimes.com/article/george-floyd-protests-timeline.html.

Ury, William. *The Third Side: Why We Fight and How We Can Stop*. New York: Penguin Group, 2000.

US Census Bureau. "Demographic Turning Points for the United States: Population Projections for 2020 to 2060," Revised February 2020. https://www.census.gov/content/dam/Census/library/publications/2020/demo/p25-1144.pdf.

Vedantam, Shankar, Parth Shah, Tara Boyle, and Tara Schmidt. "Radically Normal: How Gay Rights Activists Changed the

Minds of Their Opponents," *Hidden Brain* podcast, April 8, 2019. https://www.npr.org/2019/04/03/709567750/radically-normal-how-gay-rights-activists-changed-the-minds-of-their-opponents.

Walsh, Colleen. "Me Too founder discusses where we go from here," *The Harvard Gazette*, February 21, 2020. https://news.harvard.edu/gazette/story/2020/02/me-too-founder-tarana-burke-discusses-where-we-go-from-here/.

Wang, Amy. "Republicans Call for Unity but Won't Acknowledge Biden Won Fairly," *The Washington Post*, January 17, 2021. https://www.washingtonpost.com/politics/2021/01/17/republicans-call-unity-wont-acknowledge-biden-won-fairly/.

Wiesel, Elie. "Nobel Prize Acceptance Speech," accessed October 1, 2020. https://www.nobelprize.org/prizes/peace/1986/wiesel/26054-elie-wiesel-acceptance-speech-1986/.

Williams, David R., and Chiquita Collins. "Racial Residential Segregation: A Fundamental Cause of Racial Disparities in Health," *Race, Ethnicity, and Health: A Public Health Reader*, Thomas A. LaVeist and Lydia A. Isaac (Eds.). San Francisco: Jossey-Bass/Wiley Imprint, 2013, pp. 331–353.

Widdicombe, Lizzie. "Saturday with Greta," *The New Yorker*, April 19, 2021, p. 13.

Wolfson, Evan. "Five Years Later, How Obergefell Paved the Way for Bostock and the DACA Decision," *Slate*, June 20, 2020. https://slate.com/news-and-politics/2020/06/obergefell-fifth-anniversary-supreme-court-marriage-equality-daca.html.

Yearby, Ruqaiijah. "Racial Disparities in Health Status and Access to Healthcare: The Continuation of Inequality in the United States Due to Structural Racism," *American Journal of Economics and Sociology*, 77 (3-4), (2018): 1113–1152.

Young, Iris Marion. *Inclusion and Democracy*. New York: Oxford University Press, 2000.

Young, Iris Marion. *Justice and the Politics of Difference*. Princeton: Princeton University Press, 2011.

acknowledgments

This book draws on two different but overlapping streams of our life experiences—conflict work and social activism—and we are fortunate to have had wonderful colleagues, role models, and supporters in both. Both of us have worked with incredibly skilled conflict workers and courageous and dedicated champions of change. We have been nurtured from our very earliest years to stand up for what is right and to do so with respect for those we disagree with. We discuss some of our experiences along our journey in this book. We particularly want to acknowledge the activists who found a way of focusing their upset and anger at their experiences of oppression and turned them into meaningful movements for systemic change. These include those critical to the formation of the Black Lives Matter, Times Up, #MeToo, Colectiva Feminista en Construcción, Ricky Renuncia, and Extinction Rebellion movements. And we want to acknowledge the importance of George Floyd and his family in inspiring us to write this book.

We also want to thank the many incredible colleagues we have worked with over the years on finding a better way to deal with serious conflict. These include the many people Bernie worked with at CDR Associates, especially his long-term partners and friends Mary Margaret Golten, Chris Moore, and Susan Wildau and the current CEO, Jonathan Bartsch. Bernie would especially like to acknowledge the enduring and courageous commitment of Tom Mayer to social justice, which has been a lifelong inspiration to his little brother. Jackie has had the fortune of working with friends and colleagues at the Center for Justice and Peacebuilding at Eastern Mennonite University (EMU), including Amy C. Knorr, Jayne Docherty, David Brubaker, Gaurav Pathania, and Matt Tibbles. Jackie is also grateful to Debra Gerardi, Beryl Blaustone, Phyllis Beck Kritek, Yanira Alemán-Torres, and Mariana Hernández Crespo Gonstead for their friendship and sharing their conflict engagement wisdom and facilitation skills.

Both of us shared the experience of working together with a wonderful set of colleagues at the Negotiation and Conflict Resolution Program (originally the Werner Institute) at Creighton University. Special thanks to Mary Lee Brock, Noam Ebner, Kathy Gonzales, Amanda Guidero, Paul E. McGreal, and Palma J. Strand, with whom we discussed many of the ideas in this book as we were developing them and whose support to us at Creighton was invaluable. We are also grateful to the students whom we have had the privilege to have in our classes and whose insight and commitment to making a more just world were important to our own growth and understanding.

We received valuable assistance from many friends and colleagues in discussing our ideas and reviewing parts of this manuscript as we were developing it. Thanks to Palma J. Strand, Kathy Gonzales, Peter Adler, Howard Gadlin, Lucy Moore, Ann Gosline, Greg Bourne, David Hooker, Mary Margaret Golten, and Moya McAllister for their insightful, direct, and useful comments. We want also to acknowledge the wisdom and support of a number of allies in our efforts to confront the implicit bias that is embedded in the work we do, in particular, Susan Terry, Cheryl Jamison, Sue Bronson, Barbara Jones, Dana Caspersen, Bill Warters, TeKay Brown-Taylor, and Rachel Goldberg.

Very special thanks to Mark Mayer and Julie Macfarlane for their help in conceptualizing our fundamental message and for their insightful feedback and support from the very beginning to the very end of this effort.

We were fortunate to have two very capable partners throughout the development of our work on this book. Kezia Endsley, our editor from Wiley, provided consistently helpful, supportive, and timely feedback on the various versions of each part of this book. Katie Mulembe, a graduate student in the Center for Justice and Peacebuilding at EMU, provided invaluable commentary, editing, citation checking, and was always tactful but direct in pointing out some of our blind spots. We also want to thank the Wiley team, who grasped the value of this project and have been supportive (and flexible!) throughout—especially Jeanenne Ray, Sally Baker, Dawn Kilgore, Aldo Rosas, Manikandan Kuppan, Lori Martinsek, and Chloé Miller-Bess.

Finally, we want to thank our families for their unstinting support throughout, especially Hope Moon, Sibyl Macfarlane, Jagjit Choda, Ashley Colley, Mark Mayer, Luis Eduardo Torres Lara, Fabiana Spinelli, and Raúl Torres Lara. And our most special thanks to our partners in life and in work, whose constant willingness to listen, to support, and when necessary to distract and entertain was essential. Without you, Luis and Julie, we could not have completed this project.

about the authors

Bernie Mayer has provided conflict intervention services for families, schools, public interest groups, communities, NGOs, unions, corporations, and governmental and agencies throughout North America and internationally for over 40 years. He is professor emeritus of Conflict Studies, Creighton University, and a founding partner of CDR Associates, a conflict intervention firm headquartered in Boulder, Colorado.

Before focusing on conflict intervention, Bernie was a child and family therapist in New York City and Boulder, Colorado. He has been a long-term social activist, working on a broad array of progressive causes, including those supporting gender equality, anti-racism, environmental sustainability, and workers' rights.

Bernie received a BA from Oberlin College, an MSW from Columbia University, and a PhD from the University of Denver. He has been a prolific author of books and articles, including *The Dynamics of Conflict, Beyond Neutrality, Staying with Conflict,* and *The Conflict Paradox.* He received the 2015 John M. Haynes Distinguished Mediator Award, presented by the Association for Conflict Resolution, the 2013 President's Award, and the 2009 Meyer Elkin Award presented by the Association of Family Conciliation Courts and has twice received the CPR International Institute for Conflict Prevention and Resolution's Book of the Year Award.

Bernie lives in Kingsville, Ontario, with his wife, Julie Macfarlane.

Jacqueline (Jackie) N. Font-Guzmán is the inaugural executive director of diversity, equity, at Eastern Mennonite University and professor in their Center for Justice and Peacebuilding, Harrisonburg, Virginia. She is a Fulbright Scholar and the recipient of the 2017 Nova Southeastern University Distinguished Alumni Achievement Award. Her work has been recognized at the national and international level across disciplines.

Jackie has vast leadership and conflict experience in healthcare, academia, and the legal system. She has actively participated in the field of conflict studies and legal studies through national and international conferences. She has also conducted a wide variety of training, facilitations, and mediations throughout the United States, the Caribbean, Europe, and Latin America. She has worked with corporations, several Supreme Courts across the world, universities, healthcare institutions, and state, local, and federal agencies.

Jackie received her BA from Coe College, Cedar Rapids, Iowa, her MS in Health Care Administration from Saint Louis University, her JD degree *summa cum laude* from the Interamericana University of Puerto Rico, and her PhD in Conflict Analysis and Resolution from Nova Southeastern University, Fort Lauderdale, Florida. Her book *Experiencing Puerto Rican Citizenship and Cultural Nationalism* was selected as the Puerto Rico Bar Association 2015 Juridical Book of the Year in the category of "Essay Promoting Critical Thinking and Analysis of Juridical and Social Issues." She was also corecipient of the 2012 Madrid Mediators Association Award for Best Publication in Mediation for *Mediación y Resolución de Conflictos: Técnicas y Ámbitos*.

She lives in Harrisonburg, Virginia, with her husband, Luis A. Torres-Guerrero.

index